Form and the Art of Theatre

Form and the Art of Theatre

Paul Newell Campbell

Bowling Green State University Popular Press
Bowling Green, Ohio 43403

For material originally appearing in the *Central States Speech Journal* and the *Southern Speech Communication Journal,* acknowledgement is made to the editors of those journals.

Samuel Beckett's *A Piece of Monologue,* Copyright © 1981, is reprinted by permission of Grove Press, Inc.

To
Karlyn Kohrs Campbell

Contents

Prologue

This book is concerned with issues in the area of dramatic theory and criticism, an area that has been largely free of change in recent years. There are at least two reasons for this relative calm. First, the people who do dramatic theory and criticism are scattered through the academic world in various departments, Theatre, English, Philosophy, and others, and this dispersal makes it difficult to know and to appreciate the work that is done, even when it is brilliant work. And there is brilliant work done. Names come readily to mind: David Cole, Ruby Cohn, Francis Fergusson, Richard Gilman, Paul Hernadi, Elder Olson, Charles R. Lyons, Bert O. States, J. L. Styan, and, especially, Kenneth Burke and Susanne K. Langer, from whom I shall borrow liberally in this work. Still, there is a great difference between the efforts of individuals, no matter how important, and the frequent and fervid area-wide changes that have occurred in the theory and criticism of literature, music, and art in the last fifty years or so. Second, those theatre people who are involved in production work, in or outside the academic world, are often so consumed by the demands made on them as directors, designers, or performers that they have little energy left to devote to theory and criticism.

But beyond these obvious reasons, there is a question of interest, of attitude. A recent conference of the American Theatre Association reported, "Many individuals consider ratiocination to be harmful to creative endeavors and express reluctance to thinking/theorizing about theatre art."[1] This attitude is far from new, of course; it can probably be traced back to Plato's doctrine of inspiration, that notion of divine madness under the influence of which the artist created mindlessly. Any attempt to oppose such a view may well be futile, though the attempt has been made often enough. Northrop Frye has, perhaps, put it as bluntly as anyone:

> It is clearly the simple truth that there is no real correlation either way between the merits of art and its public reception. Shakespeare was more popular than Webster, but not because he was a greater dramatist; Keats was less popular than Montgomery, but not because he was a better poet. Consequently there is no way of preventing the critic from being, for better or worse, the pioneer of education and the shaper of cultural tradition. Whatever popularity Shakespeare and Keats have *now* is equally the result of the publicity of

1

criticism. A public that tries to do without criticism and asserts that it knows what it wants or likes, brutalizes the arts and loses its cultural memory.... The only way to forestall the work of criticism is through censorship, which has the same relation to criticism that lynching has to justice.[2]

One might add to the attempts of Frye and others the observation that anyone occupied in any way with theatre (or any of the arts) is automatically involved in theory and criticsm for the simple reason that theoretical and critical constructs inhere in language itself. Kenneth Burke writes of what he calls "terministic screens,"[3] i.e., key terms that we use in our descriptions of the world around us. He says that when we use such terms we commit ourselves to certain points of view towards the items in question; hence, "much of what we take as observations about 'reality' may be but the spinning out of possibilities implicit in our particular choice of terms."[4] And so it is with theatre. When we call something a "play," a "drama," a "tragedy," or a "comedy," we commit ourselves to whatever it is we mean by so categorizing the work. And such categorization is, of course, part of theory and criticsm. One person's criteria for what qualifies as "comedy" may differ from those of another, but each has such criteria. It is pointless to try to talk about theatre without such words, and as soon as the words are used, we are involved in theoretical and critical matters.

Theoretical *and* critical matters. The two processes are sometimes treated as separate, or at least labeled as if they were separate. In fact, they ordinarily overlap; theory involves the discussion of critical instances or examples, and criticism (at least good criticism) includes theoretical constructs and sometimes leads to new constructs.

My concern is with issues usually considered part of dramatic theory and criticsm, but I must emphasize that the object of the discussion in these pages is the *performed* work, the work as it appears on stage. Logic would dictate that I use the phrase "theatre theory and criticism" to describe my interests, and to label the two major divisions of this essay. But "dramatic theory and criticism" is used in so many courses across the country that I have chosen to avoid that terminological contest. However, the remarks in these opening pages and the titles of parts one and two aside, throughout the book I shall use the term "theatre" to mean the play in performance or in production and "drama" to mean the script, the written work. And it is *theatre* that is the focus of all that follows. This is not a matter of theatre as opposed to drama, or theatre in lieu of drama; the performed work is the playscript completed, realized, brought to life on stage. Thus, theatre includes drama.

Finally, what follows is an argument for a particular point of view toward theatre, not a summary or survey of dramatic theory and criticism, though I hope the essay includes enough references to standard sources to make it intelligible to the informed nonspecialist. My argument centers on the concept of form, a concept that is, in my judgment, the rock on which all theoretical and critical works are built, or against which they shatter. While it is by no means absent from the works of dramatic theorists and critics, the concept of form appears far more frequently in the writings of those who deal with texts than in the discourse of those who focus on performance. And I shall argue that form is the conceptual key to theatre as well as to drama.

Arguments, of course, are based on one or another sort of logic or reasoning. There are arguments that require completely specific definitions, so that if even one example can be found that does not fit the definition in every detail, the definition and all statements derived from it are invalidated. This sort of reasoning is undoubtedly necessary in some fields. However, it does not seem to me very useful in theatre, and it will not be found in these pages. To take but one example, the term "genre" cannot be defined in such a way that eleven or thirty-nine or three hundred and two criterial attributes are listed and that every item possessing those attributes belongs to genre X. And it is much the same with other notions that occupy these chapters. As a result, theatre, which is and has been a vast enterprise, obviously includes instances to which some part or another of the argument I make does not apply. That does not seem to me to be a serious matter. I mean by theatre the great, central tradition in the west that reaches from Aeschylus to Beckett. I quite understand that certain items lie outside that tradition. For instance, royal entries and progresses, mime and acrobatic displays do not seem to me to be part of theatre, though there are theatrical aspects to each of them. And even within the tradition, there are items that give me much difficulty: some of the medieval church drama, and Beckett's own *Act Without Words I* and *II*, to name but two. Recent performance events (part theatre, part music, part dance, part recitation, part TV) appear to me to be largely beyond the limits of theatre. All these are, if you will, exceptions to my argument. But my hope is that readers will agree that this is not a serious matter, that there are always exceptions, and that, in dramatic theory and criticsm as elsewhere, if the center holds much has been accomplished.

Notes

[1]"The ATA Wingspread II Conference," edited by Ronald A. Willis, *Theatre News*, 11, 9 (Summer 1979), p. 13.

[2]Northrop Frye, *Anatomy of Criticism* (New York: Atheneum, 1957), p. 4; see also pp. 4-5, 5-6. For a similar statement on the importance of theory, see R. S. Crane, *The Languages of Criticism and the Structure of Poetry* (Toronto: University of Toronto Press, 1953), p. xvi.

[3]Kenneth Burke, "Terministic Screens," in *Language as Symbolic Action: Essays on Life, Literature and Method* (Berkeley: University of California Press, 1968), pp. 44-57.

[4]Burke, p. 46.

Part I
Dramatic Theory

Chapter I

The Theatre Audience

Theatre is almost universally regarded today as a rhetorical form, i.e., one in which performers communicate with audience members and, thereby, affect them; in turn, the audience affects the performers. Given that view of theatre, it is not surprising that the audience is accepted as an essential element in the interchanges or transactions that are believed to occur between actors and audience members. The most widely held conception of the role of the audience is something like this: the audience is, in effect, one of the theatre artists; because theatre is a "living" art, because actual performers appear before actual audience members, the audience is an active participant in the live performance; as a participant, the audience experiences the performed work and responds in an immediate and emotional fashion; via that response, the audience directly affects the performance and, in fact, becomes a creative partner in the living art of theatre.

The Audience as an Essential Element of Theatre

Scholars, academic critics, newspaper reviewers, and practicing theatre artists accept the above view; they all agree that the audience is essential to theatre, and they mean artistically essential, not merely essential in a financial sense. Margot Berthold argues that the dialogue-like form of very early sepulchral inscriptions in Egypt should not be considered a forerunner of theatre because those "priestly offerings and appeals to the gods in the tomb chambers lack the decisive component of the theatre: its indispensable partner, the public."[1] J. L. Styan writes, "Playhouse, script, actors, *mise en scene*, audience are inseparable parts of the theatre event. The concept of drama put forward in this book insists that the audience has an indispensable role to play."[2] Edwin Wilson claims that "wherever we look for the fundamentals of theatre . . . we discover the primacy of the actor-audience relationship: the immediate, personal exchange whose chemistry and magic give theatre its special quality."[3] Millet and Bentley hold that "in a very real sense, a play is not a play until it is acted in a theatre before an audience."[4] Kenneth Burke says simply, "The drama, more than any other form, must never lose sight of its audience."[5] Walter Kerr puts it this way: "[Theatre] doesn't just mean that we are in the presence of the performers. It means that they are in *our* presence, conscious of us, speaking to us, working for and with us until a circuit that is not mechanical becomes established between us, a circuit that is fluid, unpredictable, ever-changing in its impulses, crackling, intimate."[6] Jerzy Grotowski makes the audience one of the two essential elements of theatre: "Can the theatre exist without an audience? At least one spectator is needed to make it a performance. . . . We can thus define the theatre as 'what takes place between spectator and actor.' "[7] So far as I can tell, there is very nearly complete agreement that the audience is essential to theatre.

The Audience as a Group

There is by no means complete agreement that, following Grotowski, a single individual can constitute an audience. Quite the contrary, the theatre audience is ordinarily considered to be a group of people and a group that responds *as* a group. No one, I believe, claims that the question of the audience is logically analogous to Bishop Berkeley's query about whether or not there is a noise if no one is present to hear the tree fall in the forest. To regard the audience in that manner would be to make the existence of the theatrical event dependent on the individual perception of that event, and on that view, theatre would exist whenever the director, or the janitor, was the sole spectator in the auditorium. Indeed, theatre would come into being whenever an actor peformed, because the actor possesses the self-awareness that allows her or him to perceive in much the way that an audience-member does. Hence, to put the question on that level is to eliminate the audience as a component of theatrical works.

Although I know of no specific number of individuals that must be present before an audience is held to exist, it is clear that the concept of audience has long been, not the individual, but a group of people who somehow manage to participate as a group in the performed work. Brecht, perhaps, puts it most strongly when he describes the audience of the commercial theatre as "a collective individual," one with "the mental immaturity and the high emotional suggestibility of a mob."[8] Of course, this is part of Brecht's argument for epic theatre and against commercial theatre, and one may, therefore, choose to discount it. But there is more than a hint of the notion of the audience as a crowd or mob in Oscar Brockett's claim that in the theatre "individuals are transformed into a group by being placed in close proximity and by sharing an experience";[9] in Brander Matthews' statement that "an audience is a crowd, and it has the special characteristics of any other crowd, of the spectators at athletic sports, of the participants in a camp-meeting, of the delegates to a political convention";[10] in Millet and Bentley's view that "spectators will influence each other's responses and, at best, will coalesce into a super-individual entity";[11] in Wilson's position that audience-members, "though still individuals, with their own personalities and backgrounds,...take on other qualities as well, qualities which often overshadow their independent response";[12] and in Elmer Rice's assertion that the theatre audience, "like any crowd, take on an identity and a character of its own, which is not wholly like that of any of its component members."[13] So, the theatre audience is thought to be essential to theatre and it behaves as a group.

The Response of the Audience

The group audience responds immediately and emotionally to the performance. This idea can be traced back to the catharsis phrase in Aristotle's definition of tragedy: "through pity and fear affecting the proper purgation of these emotions."[14] However, the catharsis phrase is notoriously difficult, and I will have more to say about it and other aspects of the *Poetics* later on.

Among moderns, Thornton Wilder says that "the theatre is directed to a group-mind," and he adds, "A group-mind presupposes, if not a lowering of standards, a broadening of the fields of interest."[15] Rice puts it bluntly:

> Of course, the appeal of the theatre is primarily emotional rather than intellectual and the effect of a play is to increase sensitivity and to blunt the power of judgment. Theatre-goers who read a play after seeing it often wonder why they were moved to laughter or to tears, or why they accepted situations and ideas that will not bear examination.[16]

Anita Block agrees and says, even more strongly: "*Theatre consciousness* is the condition of being entranced by the glamour and by the often spurious trappings of the theatre—such as clever acting, smart dialogue, dazzling costumes and effective scenery—into a drugged indifference to the values of the play content," and she adds that the judgment of the play must "be made *outside* the theatre," for "it is then and then alone, when it is presented as literature, that the values of the play can be judged."[17] In a similar vein, Altshuler and Janaro state, somewhat more mildly, "The very pleasures of theatre-going encourage the same kind of uncritical acceptance common to most spectator sports."[18] And Matthews says quite simply that "it is clear how dependent the dramatist is upon the unreflective sympathy of the spectator."[19] Hence, the audience is a necessary part of theatre, the audience behaves as a group, and audience responses are emotional responses.

The Audience's Effect on the Performance

Finally, the emotional responses of groups of audience-members directly and significantly affect the performance. Actors and directors frequently speak of the ways in which performers adapt to audiences. Henry Irving, Noel Coward, Sir Ralph Richardson, Dame Edith Evans, and Sir Laurence Olivier have talked of the differences audiences can make in performances.[20] Directors have remarked on changes in performances caused by the different audiences that see a play, for example, the interested and curious who come early in the run and the others who attend later on; they have also commented on the difference made by an audience of experts who understand the conventions employed in a particular production.[21] Those who take this position argue that theatre, as a live art, comes into existence only when the interchange between actors and audience occurs. Everything else is preparation for this. The rehearsal period is one in which a formula, a general structure, is created, but that formula or structure becomes specific only when actors and actual audiences face each other; theatre begins on opening night, the point at which the general framework becomes the specific reality that is the meeting between performers and spectators.[22] It is in these meetings, these interactions, that pauses are shortened or lengthened, that performers wait for a laugh, that timing is altered, in brief, that the actual performances are worked out beat by beat.[23]

There is widespread agreement with the view I have described. Kerr says, "*Our* presence, the way we respond, flows back to the performer and alters what he does, to some degree and sometimes astonishingly so, every night. We are contenders, making the play and the evening and the emotion together. We are playmates, building a structure."[24] Raver and Anrieu echo this claim, saying the performance is "the result of reciprocal actions and reactions in perpetual adjustment, the scene of structurings, unstructurings, and re-structurings, of building and destroying and rebuilding, of making and breaking incessantly."[25] Brockett states:

> The audience also affects the theatre through its powerful psychological impact upon performers. Actors both crave and fear audiences.... Almost all are "keyed up" because of uncertainty about the reception they will be given.... The audience, in its turn, responds to stimuli received from the production, and its reactions (in the form of rapt attention, restlessness, laughter, silence when laughter is expected) clearly affect the performers. Thus, there is constant interchange between actor and audience.[26]

Tyrone Guthrie writes that no dramatic work will "fully be brought to life until it is performed, and not unless the performance is acceptable to an audience," and he adds:

> Now the supreme thrill of the theatre is that this miracle does not always come

to pass. Sometimes the failure is the performer's fault; he may be unable to muster the physical resource, the mental concentration required. But more often it is the fault of the audience. Performance is a two-way traffic. The greatest performer can only be great when the reaction of the audience permits greatness.[27]

Perhaps these citations will suffice to show that the current and pervasive view of the theatre audience is that of a group responding emotionally to the performance and, thereby, becoming an essential part of that performance.

Empirical Data on Theatre Audiences

The view of the theatre audience I have described is so widely held, and is held by persons of such prominence, that one may advance a contradictory picture of the audience only with considerable care. Most of the items I have listed are nowadays simply accepted as part of the common sense of theatre, but it may be well to note that none of them rests on an empirical base. And yet there are some empirical data available, data which cast doubt on these common sense items.

The League of New York Theatres and Producers polled a large number of theatre-goers in and around New York City and found that, as individuals, they differed quite significantly in their responses to various theatrical techniques and in their choice of plays.[28]

In a survey of audiences of the performing arts and museums throughout New York State, it was found that, as regards theatre, 10% of the audience was 16-20 years old, 40% 21-34, 25% 35-49, 19% 50-64, and 6% 65 and over, and that ages differed as between New York City and the rest of the state; that 6% of the audience had less than a high school education, 39% less than a college education and 55% were college graduates, again with differences between the city and upstate; that 11% of the audience had incomes under $5,000, 15% $5,000-$9,999, 20% $10,000-$14,999, 25% $15,000-$24,999, and 29% $25,000 and over; that 55% of the audience was professional/executive/managerial by occupation, 15% students, 11% housewives, 12% technical/clerical/sales, 4% retired, 2% skilled/unskilled labor, and 1% other, again with differences between city and upstate audiences. It is noteworthy that in this New York study, the above percentages differed noticeably depending on whether the audience was attending a matinee, a weekday evening, or a weekend evening performance.[29]

An NEA study conducted in four southern cities focused on audience-members who go to the theatre or to symphonic concerts infrequently. The study found that such persons differed by lifestyle: 19.8% passive homebodies, 19.1% active sports enthusiasts, 14.5% inner-directed and self-sufficient, 19.8% culture patrons, 12.7% active homebodies, and 14.1% socially active.[30]

An NEA survey of 270 studies of audiences of performing arts and museums (studies that, overall, dealt with a very large sample) found that audience-members differed widely by education, by occupation, by income, and by the proportions of males and females, and the survey said in summary:

> All the variables showed considerable change from audience to audience. Some of this can be attributed to differing methodologies, such as response categories, methods of sampling, and presentation of results. Some may stem from changes within an audience. Certain characteristics of audiences were found to vary by season, time of performance (day of week, time of day), and the particular content of the performance or exhibit. One final source of variation is that the composition of the audience appears to differ slightly for different art forms.... Among the performing arts, theatre audiences were somewhat less educated and less wealthy, and they were composed of a smaller proportion of professionals than audiences for the other performing art forms.[31]

William Gourd found marked differences in the perception of plays and of the characters in them as between "cognitively simple" and "cognitively complex" audience-members.[32]

David Addington surveyed audience studies and discovered important differences among members of given audiences.[33]

Kase, Sikes, and Speilberger found that boys and girls reacted with different degrees of anxiety to the threatening content of story theatre productions.[34]

Mulac and Rudd discovered that the regional dialects of speakers had effects on audience-members who used those same dialects that were quite different from the effects on audience-members who did not use those dialects.[35]

Implications of these Empirical Data

These studies vary widely and one must deal with the findings somewhat cautiously. The Gourd and Addington studies, e.g., are by theatre people and of theatre audiences, and they directly address the issue of differences among individual audience-members and among audiences as groups. Others, e.g., the Kase, Sikes, and Spielberger and the Mulac and Rudd studies are less pertinent; the first is a study of children, and the second is a study of nontheatre audiences, but both have implications for theatre. Still others, e.g., the studies of audiences in New York and the two NEA studies do not often deal directly with the matter of what individuals or groups do, think, or feel in the theatre; for the most part, they quantify such items as age differences, educational differences, income differences, etc.; but these studies are, *in toto*, of extraordinarily large numbers of people, and there comes a point at which one feels justified in inferring that eighteen year old students who have just finished high school and are attending the theatre for only the third time will respond differently than the fifty-five year old writers or professors who have been theatre buffs for a quarter of a century.

Empirical studies of theatre audiences have been relatively few in number, but on two issues the results are, I believe, conclusive: *audience-members differ as individuals, and audiences differ as groups.* These are not startling findings, and they are buttressed by common sense, an untrustworthy ally on occasion, but one whose support is often comforting. What is significant here is that these findings work directly against the usual view of the theatre audience.

Part of the evidence directly supports the idea that individuals respond differently to what they see on stage, and part supports that idea only indirectly. But when one combines the data on actual differences in individual responses (the Gourd, Addington, and League of New York Theatres and Producers studies) with the data on differences in age, education, occupation, general interests, life-style, theatre-going habits, etc., one is forced to conclude that audiences do not, in fact, behave simply as groups, the common belief to the contrary notwithstanding. This conclusion deals a severe blow to the typical picture of the theatre audience: for one thing, a performance can never be aimed at or designed for an actual audience of theatre-goers, for a performance is, after all, one performance, not two or twenty or two hundred different performances presented to different individuals; for another, the audience cannot affect the performance in the simple fashion usually imagined, for the audience-members will respond in many and various ways, and those responses will often interfere with and even contradict one another.

Nor is it true that, though audience-members differ as individuals, audiences are somehow the same when considered as groups. Both individual and group differences occur along ranges, so that one audience may be made up of individuals who are relatively theatre-wise but who differ in their attitudes toward the classics vs. the avant-garde, another audience may consist of individuals who have different theatre-going backgrounds but who generally prefer the classics to the avant-garde, and still another of those who differ both in theatre experience and in their choice of plays. One could describe example after example, each of which included important differences among individuals and among groups. Because audiences differ as groups, the responses of those groups will also differ, as in the case of audiences from New York City and those from upstate, or audiences attending matinee, evening, or weekend performances.

By definition, performances are unable to take into account differences among individual audience-members. For quite different reasons, they are also unable to take into account group differences. For instance, it would be impossible to gather information as to what particular audience was present on a given night. And if that information could be gathered and disseminated, performances would have to differ quite significantly in order to be adapted to the actual audience on a particular evening. The characters would be developed differently, different blocking would be used, the business would differ; it would amount to having a number of performances ready and choosing one for each audience. Note that this is not a question of asking that a company be prepared to present all important *interpretations* of a play; rather, it is a question of *adapting* a particular interpretation to given audiences. For example, a director might interpret *The Time of Your Life* in such a way that Nick's bar becomes a haven offering protection from most of the world's evils, a place of warmth and friendship in which Joe is a somewhat mysterious figure around whom the others cluster. This interpretation might then be adapted to an audience that wanted to do but little of its own work, that wanted easy laughter, by emphasizing the comic aspects of such characters as Willie and Harry and by making Joe the fond protector of all; the same interpretation might be adapted to a more sophisticated audience by emphasizing the ambiguity of Joe's character and by making Willie and Harry (and the others, the Arab, Kit Carson, the Drunkard, the Society Couple), not comic characters, but eccentrics and by depending on the audience to work out the meanings thus performed.

In very practical terms, adapting performances to actual audiences would mean using significantly different characterizations, blocking, line-readings, etc., and that means that more time, talent, energy, and money would be required than are available in the real world of theatre. Further, differences in these adaptations would inevitably involve differences in lighting, costume, make-up, and set design, and changing these elements of technical theatre at the last moment before a performance would be quite impossible.

The available empirical data and the inferences based on them deny what has been believed to be the simple, direct contact between actors and audience. If those watching plays differ as individuals and as groups and, therefore, respond differently to performances, then theatrical works are anything but the straightforward transactions between performers and audience-members they have been thought to be, and performances are not, cannot be, prepared for or adapted to those actual persons who fill the house. And if the theatre ignores audience differences, then to precisely that extent performances are not directed toward actual audiences, and it cannot be claimed that actual audiences are artistic partners in the theatrical event.

Theatre Audiences and Theatre Artists,
Music and Dance Audiences

And there are additional troublesome issues, further reasons to doubt the conventional picture of the theatre audience. Beyond the empirical data that work against the ordinary view of the theatre audience, there are logical implications in that view that make it even more problematic. These implications have to do with the relationships assumed to exist between the theatre audience and other theatre artists and between the theatre audience and music and dance audiences.

The common view of the theatre audience makes it the *only* participant in the theatrical work permitted to respond emotionally on the basis of the experience of the moment. For anyone else, spontaneous, emotional response would be at best unsatisfactory, at worst ludicrous, as a basis for involvement in the theatrical event. No one would expect an actor to do expert work in a cold reading, no matter how much he or she liked the play, no matter how intensely he or she experienced the work in that reading. Even less would one expect a director or designer to work on the basis of some spontaneous, emotional reaction; for them, the lack of careful preparation would be deadly. Yet the audience, as ordinarily conceived, is expected to properly understand and evaluate the performed work, no matter how difficult it is, and to do so on the basis of one, unprepared, cold hearing. Thus, it is clear that far less is demanded of audiences by way of training and preparation than of actors, directors, or designers. If audiences are, indeed, artistic partners, if they are essential to performances, the logic of the matter will require that the creative abilities of the playwright, director, actors, designers, *and audiences* must somehow match, at least approximately, for if the performance is markedly above or below the audience's artistic powers, the result will be failure. I am not concerned at this point with the issue of elitism in the theatre. If the Neil Simon comedy requires little of the audience, so be it; but if the Beckett piece is taxing, the audience must be able to meet its demands. The question is whether or not an immediate, emotional audience response can meet the requirements of the Simon comedy *and* the Beckett play, of the Broadway musical *and* the Shakespearean drama. Such responses are inadequate when they come from directors, designers, and actors, and the idea that the audience is somehow more gifted than other theatre workers is hardly convincing.

The second bothersome implication in the common view of the theatre audience involves a comparison between the audiences of theatre, music, and dance. It can come as something of a surprise to realize that theatre is the sole performing art to grant prominence to the audience and its reponses. One can hardly imagine a music critic arguing that the success or failure of a Rachmaninoff concerto depended on the audience's reaction. Or a dance critic claiming that a Fokine ballet was good or bad because the audience did or did not creatively particpate. Natalia Makarova's 1980 staging of *La Bayadère* received considerable attention, none of it focused on the audience. Articles were written about her ability as a choreographer,[36] about the difference between this and the Petipa version,[37] and about the effects achieved by the dancers appearing in the principal roles.[38] Critics appraised the work differently, but all of their criticism was of the ballet and the performances thereof. There was no mention of the audience as a creative partner; indeed, there was almost no mention of the audience. And that is not at all unusual. Anna Kisselgoff, perhaps the finest dance critic writing today, regularly emphasizes issues concerning the structure of a ballet and/or its performance, but she makes almost no reference to audiences.[39]

It is the same with music. Harold C. Schonberg, for example, consistently ignores the audience in his criticism. Arguing the old issue of "program" versus "absolute" music, he had almost nothing to say about the audience.[40] Even with opera, the musical form most closely related to theatre, Schonberg concentrates on the musical work; his analysis of Schubert's rarely performed *Fierrabras* was devoted entirely to the musical form, with not a word about the audience.[41] In music, this emphasis on form is not limited to the classics, but extends to the middle ranges of the avant-garde. Recently, a critic described one contemporary musical work as involving a performer "wandering about the gallery making mostly mournful noises on his trombone"; another "responded to those noises with gentle electronic noises of his own," and "after 35 minutes of this, [the first performer] wandered by the console and attached a small microphone to his instrument" so that "his notes triggered a microcomputer that in turn affected the synthesized sounds. . . . This made for a less radical break from the first piece to the second and helped to lend the concert a unity it might otherwise have lacked."[42] No matter whether one regards this kind of thing as serious music or as sheer nonsense, it is evident that there is some concern for formal properties of the music; the comment about a less radical break between the two pieces and about unity in the concert shows an interest in musical form, not in the audience's ability or lack of it.

It is not until one turns to theatre or reaches the extreme edges of the avant-garde in music and dance that the audience is made a significant element in the work. Schonberg argues that the distinction between opera and musical comedy rests largely on the fact that operas are composed in accord with the author's own artistic dictates, "not the dictates of immediate audience success," while musical comedy "is carefully tested for audience reaction on the road. Songs or ensembles, no matter how brilliantly composed, are ruthlessly discarded if they do not work—that is, if audiences do not immediately respond."[43] It will be noted that it is the move from music to theatre that brings the audience into mention. And in the extreme reaches of the avant-garde, where one may find a piece of music that is a 60 cycle hum prolonged "eternally" or a dance piece that consists of simple gestures, one discovers that the audience is again important. In these sorts of work, it is often "performance artists" who display their talents, not dancers, musicians, or actors; and the efforts of these performance artists "would not be possible unless the level of overt technical virtuosity were low."[44] But low though it may be, this lack of virtuosity has a beneficial effect on the audience, according to one critic, who writes of such "blank art":

> It is clearly a part of the prevalent anti-intellectualism and nonverbalism of the times, and just as clearly related—somehow—to the drug experience.... Not all blank artists are stoned when they create or perform, and not all audiences have to alter their consciousnesses artificially before a full appreciation of this work is possible. Still, the marijuana high is a contemplative one for many people,...a central one for our sensibility, and most people seem to be able to recall that mode of thinking at will.[45]

At this point, I have, of course, moved the argument into an area that invites ridicule: create together while stoned together. I cite this particular, bizarre case, not to show that any and every emphasis on audience response leads to such views of art and the appreciation of art, but simply to indicate the nature of the audience reaction postulated in the fringes of the avant-garde.

It all seems to come down to this: If it is, indeed, true that theatre audiences experience the performed work in some direct fashion, if they respond immediately on the basis of that experience, and if their responses are themselves important parts of the theatrical event, that means that theatre audiences are quite unlike the theatre artists for whom discipline and training are essential *and* quite unlike the audiences of music and dance who are not regarded as indispensable elements of the performances they observe. Theatre, dance, and music are all performing arts. How is it that, alone among audiences and among theatre artists, the theatre audience is able to experience the artwork so significantly that its immediate response is thought to be essential to that artwork? To the best of my knowledge, no explanation of the audience's ability has been given, and I suggest that a view of the theatre audience that requires so exalted a function is, by definition, an unlikely one.

Yet it is not enough to argue against the traditional view of the theatre audience; one must suggest an alternative, and I will try to do so by turning again to the arts of music and dance.

The Virtual Audience

With music and dance audiences, what is required is not merely an experience, but knowledge, training, and dedication to the art. It is never assumed that the artwork must come to the audience, but always that the audience will somehow accomodate itself to the artwork. At times, quite an extraordinary amount of knowledge or ability is demanded of the audience. For example, in some of the criticism of the Makarova version of *La Bayadère*, very complicated points about the differences between this and the Petipa production are made.[46] Now, Marius Petipa's original version was presented in 1877, well before present viewers were born. Hence, Makarova's work is not only regarded as apart from the audience's simple experience of it, but is examined from a vantage point of considerable historical knowledge, knowledge that could have been attained only by study of the art form. Implicit in this criticism is the idea that an appropriate concept of the ballet is being presented, and the knowledge necessary to an understanding of that concept is simply taken for granted; there is not the slightest indication in this or other dance (or music) criticism that the audience response is a substitute for knowledge of the artwork. Rather, it is assumed that the work is intended for an experienced audience, a dedicated audience.

Quite the same thing is expected of theatre artists, of directors, actors, and designers. Both for them and for music and dance audiences, what is necessary is not merely an experience of the moment, but experience in the form of study of the script (or score), exposure to other works by the author and other works in the genre, and experience of the theatre (music, dance) in general. What is wanted in each case is not experience resulting in an immediate response, but experience filtered through a great deal of training and prior study, i.e., a *mediate* response.

It may be wondered, I suppose, whether or not I am asking the impossible. Am I hinting at some sort of censorship of theatre audiences? Guards at the doors to check artistic I.Q. cards? Perhaps a system of accumulated points, with theatre-goers earnestly struggling to compile the magic number that will admit them to a *serious* work?

Of course not, for this very important reason: The theatre artists I have mentioned are actual persons who actually work in productions, as are the composers, choreographers, and performers of music and dance. But the music and dance audiences assumed in the criticism I have referred to are not actual, but abstract or virtual audiences, i.e., critical concepts designed to make it possible to talk about music and dance more profitably. When great sophistication is demanded of music and dance audiences, that does not mean that actual audience-members always possess that sophistication; such highly skilled audiences are abstract, not actual groups. By contrast, in the theatre we talk of actual audiences. There may, of course, be some differences between the actual audiences of music and dance and those of theatre, as I have already indicated. Such differences are at least suggested by the fact that language is an important element of theatre and is a natural symbology, while the symbologies of music and dance are artificial and must be learned. But there is no evidence that the differences between theatre and music/dance audiences are radical. The large NEA survey found that "in terms of educational attainment, the museum visitors and performing arts audiences surveyed were far more similar to one another than either group was to the general public."[47] The study of New York State audiences concluded that "theatre audiences do differ, though only marginally, from audiences at opera and symphony/classical music. They are more heavily female, somewhat younger, but still well educated and affluent, though to a somewhat lesser degree than opera and symphony/classical music audiences.... All in all, theatre audiences do not differ drastically from serious music audiences, although they appear to be a somewhat less elite group."[48] There is, then, no evidence that commits one to the ill-considered conclusion that, somehow, actual music and dance audiences are made up of highly gifted persons, while theatres are filled with dullards. There are undoubtedly musical illiterates who go to concerts; there are those who know and care little about dance who will be found watching Baryshnikov and Twyla Tharp; and there are those in theatre audiences who have minimal cognitive and aesthetic abilities. These people will always be with us. The great difference is not between the actual audiences of theatre and music/dance; the difference is that, although music and dance have their share of audience incompetents, they do not handicap themselves by making actual audiences, incompetents included, essential parts of their artworks. And it is time, I think, to follow their lead and to work with the notion of an abstact or virtual theatre audience.

That notion fits easily enough into the reality of theatre, for theatrical performances have their own objective existence on stage, as do those of music and dance, and are not dependent on some particular audience, or on any audience at all. In the real world of theatre, the director uses the rehearsal period to prepare and polish one and only one performance.

That performance is then presented to each audience that comes into the house. Changes occur from one performance to another, of course, but those changes fall readily into three categories. First, there are the critically insignificant differences. An actor may take a long cross from one side of the stage to the other, and the arc may differ by an inch or two from night to night. The volume level for one scene may be just a hair higher or lower on this or that evening. Or the tempo in a long speech may vary by just a shade in some performances. Audiences do not perceive such differences, though actors, director, and stage manager may on occasion. But perceived or not, these changes do not affect the form of the theatrical work. They are, after all, critically insignificant differences. Second, there are accidents. They are critically significant, surely, but in a very odd way. One excuses them if they occur rarely enough and if they are unquestionably accidents. A flat may fall over, a spot light blow out, or an actor stumble and fall down. In a great surge of suspension of disbelief, one will work determinedly to keep the accident from spoiling the scene. But if the accidents occur too often, or if there is the likelihood that they could have been prevented somehow, the production is lost, quite as it would be if the incidents were intentional. And third, there are the critically significant differences in line readings, in movement, in the crispness of scene changes and light cues, even in characterization. When such differences occur in any number or severity, one simply writes off the production as a poor one. For the sign of the well-prepared production is that its performances do not vary greatly, but are marked by consistency. One has but to ask the stage manager of any long-running show how much the playing-time varies from evening to evening to be aware of the striking sameness of the performances.

Actual audiences exist, of course, and their behaviors change, too. Sometimes they will laugh, sometimes be silent, sometimes rustle their programs and fidget, and by such actions they undoubtedly communicate their pleasure or displeasure to the actors. And in certain very limited ways, the actors will respond to the audience; e.g., they will wait for applause or laughter to die down. But the form of the work does not change, nor do the great majority of the details of that work. All the technical elements remain constant, of course. So does the blocking, and so do the characterizations. And even minor changes in timing are sharply limited. For instance, if a single actor changes her or his rhythm or tempo to any great degree, it will throw an entire scene out of balance; and if all the actors in the scene change the tempo, the entire play can be pushed off center. True, actors may use somewhat more energy if the audience is inattentive or noisy, but in a good production the timing of the piece is essentially unchanged. The over-all tempo of the play, the speed with which cues are picked up, the slowing down of certain lines, the use of pauses—all these elements of timing are decided on and then carefully polished in the rehearsal period.[49] To make all such matters part of the relationship or interchange between actors and actual audiences is to invite chaos.

And chaos threatens from another direction if one takes seriously the idea that audiences are artistic partners in the theatrical event and significantly affect performances. If that is true, it is impossible to talk meaningfully about *Hamlet* or even a particular production of *Hamlet*. Because each performance changes as a result of audience participation, we will have to talk about the performance of *Hamlet* by this or that company on this or that evening. And that means that the worlds of theatre and of dramatic criticism will be crowded with thousands, even tens of thousands, of *Hamlets*, *Lears*, and *Godots*, and the entire critical and creative process will grind to a halt. *For it is necessary to talk about a play:* necessary for the critic and theorist, of course, but just as necessary for the designer or director or actor who approaches the play as something more than an unexamined rush of emotion.

Clearly, we do not find it impossible to talk about *Hamlet*. We say that such and such a performance or a set design was right or wrong *for the play*, and we have something in mind when we say *for the play*. The matter is complicated because, from the point of view of theatre, "the play" is an abstraction that grows out of the script and out of a certain number (perhaps a very large number) of productions of that script. But to multiply the complications by holding that within each production particular performances are to be distinguished because different audiences responded differently and, thereby, helped create different works of art is to strain credulity. We may *say* that the audience functions in this fashion, but we do not observe that preachment in our theatrical practices. Hence, I am arguing for a change, not in practice, but in what we say about the theatre.

It is the quality of the one performance put together in rehearsal that constitutes the art of theatre, but then, of course, there comes that special time called opening night, and one may as well deny the phases of the moon as question its special status. Its electricity is surely due in a very real sense to that house full of moving, muttering, live human beings. But it does not follow that those live human beings make up the audience the actors are prepared to play to. Indeed, the actors may very well feel excitement, or panic, at the sight of all those faces and still be ready to perform only for an audience quite unlike the one sitting there. There is an obvious difference between rehearsal and opening night, but the fact is that opening night does not mark the beginning of theatre. This point becomes clear, I believe, when one considers a commonplace experience that occurs during the rehearsal period, usually in the final week or two of rehearsals.

One can be sitting in the dark house with no other person (or at most one or two others) present and find that things suddenly work, that a line is read just a bit differently, a pause is held a moment longer, the actors look at each other with new eyes, the whole scene comes to life, and the magic of theatre is palpable in the empty house. A theatrical form has appeared. And for that it was not necessary for an audience to be present. While the excitement of opening night is utterly real, so is the magic that pervades the empty auditorium. Thus, it is not the existence of the audience that is the test, the mark of theatre; what counts is that sure awareness that sends prickles up one's spine, and it counts no matter whether one is alone or in the middle of a full house.

Support for the Concept of the Virtual Audience

Though not widely held by theatre people, the idea of a virtual audience is not new, and in other arts it is very nearly a commonplace. David Young says, "We must grant the dramatist the same privileges we grant the novelist and the poet—an ideal auditor, reader, or spectator."[50] And in regard to literature, Don Geiger writes:

> Even superior work which seems to "address" a particular audience—one recalls, for example, Pope's satires, the occasional poetry of Dryden, even some of the work of Shakespeare—is memorable, we think, because it was so well formed that it transcended its local purpose. Much of the worst of these—and other—writers' work is bad, we suppose, just because it was so particularly "addressed" to some particular audience.[51]

And Northrop Frye has this to say:

> Poetry is a *disinterested* use of words: it does not address a reader directly. When it does so, we usually feel that the poet has some distrust in the capacity of readers and critics to interpret his meaning without assistance and has therefore dropped into the sub-poetic level of metrical talk ("verse" or "doggerel") which anybody can learn to produce.[52]

In regard to theatre, this same idea (in somewhat different form) is voiced by Stanislavski:

> Do not belittle our art. Are we to be merely agents, middlemen, between the playwright and the public? No, we are creators in our own right. And does our creativeness consist of no more than reading a role to the public and conversing with it? On the stage we live first for ourselves, because we have the ability to desire to live by the emotions of a part and the ability to share them with those who are living on the stage with us. As for the spectator, he is an accidental witness. Speak up so that he can hear you, place yourself in the right parts of the stage so that he can see you, but for the rest, forget entirely about the audience and put your mind solely on the characters in the play. It is not for the actor to be

interested in the spectator, but the other way around: the spectator should be
engrossed in the actor.[53]

Stanislavski is not arguing here for the concept of an abstract audience, of
course, at least not directly. But his words are entirely hospitable to that
concept, whereas they offer little support for the notion of actual audiences
that affect the performances actors give. The description of the spectator as
accidental witness certainly seems to make impossible the role of creative
partner in the work.

Supporting evidence comes from other major figures, too. Brecht,
whose alienation theory placed enormous importance on the audience, did
not talk of individual audiences altering performances. And Artaud, who
wanted to assault the audience, did not advocate one sort of assault for this
audience, another for that one. But most striking of all, support comes
from Aristotle.

I mentioned earlier the catharsis phrase in the *Poetics* as the source of
the idea that audiences respond emotionally, but the handling of emotions
by Aristotle is not nearly so simple as one might think. Aristotle did not
speak of the feelings as being opposed to the intellect. Butcher points out
that, in Aristotle's philosophical system, "the end of an object is inherent
in that object and is reached when the object has achieved its specific
excellence and fulfils the law of its own being."[54] There appears to be a
contradiction when, for the art of tragedy, Aristotle "assumes a subjective
end consisting in a certain pleasurable emotion."[55] But while Butcher does
not deny the inconsistency here, he does not find it a major one, for he
emphasizes:

> In Aristotle the true nature of a thing can be expressed by means of that which it
> is "capable of doing or suffering" ($\pi\acute{\epsilon}\phi\upsilon\kappa\epsilon \ \pi\upsilon\iota\epsilon\iota\upsilon \ \pi\acute{\alpha}\sigma\chi\epsilon\iota\upsilon$).
> Its effect is treated as synonymous with its essential quality. So it is in a work of
> art. If indeed we desire to characterise precisely its emotional effect we must do
> so by reference to the content of the activity. But the work of art and its effect
> being inseparable, the artistic object can loosely be spoken of in terms of the
> emotion it awakens. This view does not, however, make the function of art to
> depend upon accident and individual caprice. The subjective emotion is deeply
> grounded in human nature, and thence acquires a kind of objective validity.[56]

And Butcher makes it quite clear that Aristotle is not talking of audience
responses in the modern sense (or, indeed, of the response of actual
audiences):

> In fine, the end of any art is not "any chance pleasure," but the pleasure which is
> distinctive of the art. To the ideal spectator or listener, who is a man of educated

taste and represents an instructed public, every fine art addresses itself; he may be called "the rule and standard" of that art, as the man of moral insight is of morals: the pleasure that any given work of art can afford to him is the end of the art....

Though the end, then, is a state of feeling, it is a feeling that is proper to a normally constituted humanity. The hedonistic effect is not alien to the essence of art, as has sometimes been thought; it is the subjective aspect of a real objective fact. Each kind of poetry carries with it a distinctive pleasure, which is the criterion by which the work is judged. A tragic action has an inherent capacity of calling forth pity and fear; this quality must be impressed by the poet on the dramatic material; and if it is artistically done, the peculiar pleasure arising out of the union of the pitiable and the terrible will be awakened in the mind of every one who possesses normal human sympathies and faculties.[57]

Gerald F. Else argues even more strongly that the notion of catharsis should be understood to refer, not to subjective responses, but to formal and structural elements in the play:

Thus the catharsis is not a change or end-product in the spectator's soul, or in the fear and pity (i.e., the dispositions to them) in his soul, but a process carried forward in the emotional material of the play by its structural elements, above all by the recognition. For the recognition is...the hinge on which the emotional structure of the play turns. The catharsis, that is, the purification of the tragic act by the demonstration that its motive was not μιαρον is accomplished by the whole structure of the drama, but above all by the recognition.[58]

All this is, of course, a far cry from the present notion of audiences responding in particular ways and, thereby, affecting performances. While neither Else nor Butcher denies the existence of actual audiences in Aristotle's scheme of things, each reads Aristotle as concerned with the form of the theatrical work and, to the extent that an audience is involved, with an ideal audience.

Aristotle's theory of tragedy operates only within some certain limits. But even though the *Poetics* cannot be taken as the definitive theory of drama from the classical period to the present, it is certainly the most significant single work in dramatic theory. And it is important to realize that the concept of an actual theatre audience that helps create the theatrical form has no foundation in the *Poetics*.

In sum, theatre is in reality very much like dance and music; the performed works that make up the world of theatre have a formal and objective existence, and those works are prepared and presented in as expert and as uniform a manner as possible to the various audiences that attend. Still, we will inevitably think of each performance as intended for an audience. And, of course, it is. But that target audience, like the audiences of music and dance, is an abstract, an experienced, a knowledgeable, a well-tempered audience, if you will. In brief, a virtual audience. Such virtual audiences will be perfectly matched by actual audiences rarely or never. But the value of the concept of the virtual audience is not that it can be used to describe or lead one to actual audiences, but that it allows one to deal with the artwork with more understanding and more grace.

The Choice of Virtual Audiences

Lest I be thought to have overstated the case, let me say once more that there *are* actual audiences that see plays. And actual audience-members on occasion behave oddly and even disrupt the evening's proceedings. If, for example, a block of tickets has been sold to an organization whose members travel to the theatre by bus, if the bus breaks down, and if a crowd of people comes scurrying into the theatre in the middle of the first act, that can surely interfere with the concentration of the actors (*and* the audience). If a drunk talks loudly or becomes obstreperous, that, too, can upset actors and audience-members. Such things happen, and I certainly do not deny it. It is simply that I believe such events are not to be considered the basis on which a theory of theatre art and its relationship to the audience is to be constructed. Happenings of the sort are outside the norm of audience behavior. There is, of course, the interesting matter of whether or not that norm is changing, but, so far as I know, there are too few data available for a meaningful answer to be given. And, in any event, that is quite another question.

More important than the aberrant audience behaviors suggested above are the attempts on the part of playwrights, directors, and actors to make contact with actual audiences. A number of those attempts took place in the 1960s, and while they are important as part of the history of theatre, there is little evidence that they have become permanent parts of the art of theatre. The Living Theatre's *Paradise Now* is, perhaps, the best example of this sort of work: a long, aggressive, episodic event that attempted to push the audience into revolutionary action, *Paradise Now* had actors roam through the audience, talking to individuals, arguing with them, insulting them, even spitting in their faces; of course, the audience was not provoked into revolution, and there is no indication that *Paradise Now* was a political force in its era.[59]

Other attempts to play to actual audiences have occurred more or less within the mainstream of theatre, and these, too, are instructive. By an odd coincidence, I saw what are within my own experience the two most extreme such attempts on successive evenings, this in forty-some years of theatre-going. The 1977 Theatre Guild production of *Golda*, by William

Gibson, directed by Arthur Penn, and starring Anne Bancroft was an unimportant theatre piece. An episodic work that narrated Israel's difficulties facing many Arab enemies and her trials in wartime, the play's major attraction was Anne Bancroft's technically brilliant impersonation of Golda Meir. But the audience was responsible for creating an extraordinary evening in the theatre. The curtain had not been up for five minutes when I realized that something unusual was happening; nobody was kicking the back of my seat, programs were not being rustled, there was no whispering, and for minutes at a time there was not even the sound of a single cough. This audience was watching and listening and doing it intensely, almost reverently. And at the end of the show, quite an amazing thing happened. Having led her country through a time of troubles, the Golda Meir character turns to the audience and says that she will leave them with one word, the best of all. And then Bancroft said, perhaps six or eight times, and directing it to various parts of the house, "Shalom! Shalom! Shalom! Shalom!..." After the second or third repetition, I began to hear murmurs coming back from the audience, "Shalom! Shalom!" It was an electrifying moment, and the thought flashed into my mind, "They're saying 'Peace!' to Golda Meir, not to Anne Bancroft." My assumption was, and is, that many or most of the audience-members were Jews, people vitally interested in Israel as a homeland, not simply a country. But whoever they were, they created a most unusual evening in the theatre, an evening of social and political, and even religious, dedication. Unfortunately, the play remained a work of little importance.

The next night, I saw Joseph Papp's production of "Miss Margarida's Way," written and directed by Roberto Athayde and starring Estelle Parsons. This was a novelty piece, a one-person show in which a substitute teacher talks to a grade-school class. The play opened at Papp's Public Theatre in the Village and got good reviews; it was then moved uptown to the Ambassador, and a fairly heavy publicity campaign encouraged audiences to come and take part in the play. Take part they did, with a vengeance. Estelle Parsons had but to invite responses and they were immediately called out, some of them harmless enough. But quite soon, halfway or so through the first act, the audience became ugly. The comments had nothing to do with what was happening on stage, but were apparently designed to please those uttering them. And the utterers produced such imaginative remarks as, "Hey, Margarida, ya' screwin' the principal" and "Ah, fuck you!" I was shocked. Not at the obscenities, but at the deliberate destruction of what at least claimed to be an artwork. The play, of course, invited destruction and in that sense deserved what it got; there was the publicity that urged people to participate, and the script had the substitute teacher behaving absurdly, using obscenities of her own, throwing her legs in the air and exposing her crotch. Still, I could not help wondering what a *Golda* audience might have made of *"Miss Margarida's Way."* Suppose the audience-members had seriously tried to put themselves in the role of seventh graders. Might there have been an interesting interchange between stage and virtual audience? Well, probably not, for the very notion of a thousand or more people somehow agreeing to play the roles of seventh grade children indicates the near-impossibility of the task.

The two experiences demonstrated with extraordinary clarity the extremes of audience behavior, the one beneficent, the other malevolent. But neither created, or even added to, the play being presented. The *Golda* audience created a moving experience, but it did not make *Golda* a better play. And the other audience destroyed whatever values *"Miss Margarida's Way"* possessed as a playscript.

By comparison, the New York productions of *A Chorus Line* and *Equus* were adapted to the best possible virtual audiences, i.e., the best of the virtual audiences to which those works could appeal. In both cases, expert and stylish staging techniques covered up quite serious problems in the scripts. And with both productions, one was treated to one of the unique functions of theatre as an art form, the ability to treat a dramatic work so that its strengths are made prominent and its weaknesses hidden, a kind of artistic obfuscation, if you will.

Always, it is a virtual audience toward which a performance is aimed. But the question remains as to which of the available virtual audiences a particular production will select. There are, after all, many virtual audiences. And here I *am* concerned with the issue of elitism in theatre, for that issue now enters in such a way that it cannot be ignored. Virtual audiences fall naturally into a scale, a rank order. At the top is the audience of knowledgeable and practiced theatre-goers who prepare themselves for the performance, who have finely honed aesthetic abilities, whose view of their fellow beings is marked by understanding, and whose tastes are catholic. For many (but certainly not all) works, such an audience is a director's and an actor's dream, though that dream may be realized rarely or never in an entire career. All other audiences are increasingly imperfect realizations of that dream, and at the furthest remove from it lies the group composed of people unfamiliar with the script, inexperienced in theatre, unwilling to exert themselves imaginatively, suspicious of their fellow humans, and possessed of fixed and narrow tastes. The principle problem in peforming for a virtual audience of the first sort is simply that not every work is good enough, nor every director, actor, or designer gifted enough to appeal to it; the major problem with an audience of the second sort is that any work of signifcant power and worth will be damaged and weakened if it is bent to the needs of such a group. (I speak of the extremes, but most audiences selected will, of course, fall somewhere in the virtual middle.)

Because differences among virtual audiences fall into this sort of order, the choice of any one of them is the choice of a certain level of audience ability, and therefore, a choice inevitably associated with the issue of elitism. Not the radical elitism that denies a place in the theatre to any audience not expert in dealing with all plays, but the modest elitism that requires that justice be done to the artwork by presenting the chosen interpretation of that work to the best of the virtual audiences for which that play is suitable. The adaptation aimed at the most able of virtual audiences must be the one the production mounts, and on this view, there is room in the theatre for the most demanding works and for the most thorough-going instances of sheer entertainment.

One brief example of a production that chose the wrong virtual audience: The 1979 Broadway production of *Richard III*, with Al Pacino as Richard, was not a success. The Schubert organization announced that there would be no formal opening-night because, as Bernard Jacobs said, Pacino "does not want to perform before a typical opening-night audience. This is a play for people under 45. Al gets an average audience between 15 and 25 years old. He wants his young people there who understand what he is doing."[60] Although the critics found the production a shambles (Kerr said, "We end up not so much with *Richard III* as with Richard of Third Avenue."[61]), Jacobs claimed that "Al gives a very specific interpretation of the part. He's not Gielgud. He's not Richardson. His purpose in doing this play is to develop a young audience for Shakespeare. He has accomplished this, if nothing else."[62] It is hard to imagine a more direct admission of unconcern for actual audiences; even the statistical average, between 15 and 25, ignores all those audience-members outside the age span. By their own testimony, the people who controlled this production aimed at a particular virtual audience, not the actual persons who attended. That, I would argue, is inevitable, but my objection here is that the virtual audience for which this production was designed was, on all the evidence, far below the natural demands of the material. While Pacino and his producers may have created an audience for something, it was far more likely for Pacino than for Shakespeare. It is in such cases as this, when the material is lowered to an audience that cannot rise to the material, that the result is severely weakened plays.[63]

The theatre cannot gear its productions to actual audiences. At the same time, the theatre cannot present unfocused performances aimed at no audience at all. Every performance is prepared for and presented to some virtual audience, for no matter what audience is chosen, it will be an abstraction of the audience that actually takes its place in the house. What remains, then, is to present each work at its best by assuming that the finest and most appreciative of the virtual audiences for that play will be the audience out front. If that is not done, if the tie between actor and actual audience is emphasized, the all-important three-way relationship between play-actor-(virtual) audience is destroyed, and one is forced into untenable critical positions, for instance that the Pacino *Richard III* was successful because the 15-year-olds liked the actor. Some plays are difficult and complex forms, others absurdly simple; they may be interpreted variously when they are brought to life in a production, and once an interpretation is decided upon it can be adapted to different virtual audiences. But it is at just that point that the demands of the play must be considered, for the simple fact is that the abilities of actual audiences do not always match the requirements of the work performed. Hence, the choices made at that juncture determine whether the play (in the interpretation decided upon) will be damaged by adaptation to an audience unable to meet its demands, or will be renewed by a performance designed for a virtual audience competent to deal with the artwork.

I have devoted this entire chapter to, have perhaps belabored, a single issue, namely, the idea that theatre consists of artworks that have their own formal and objective existence on stage. There are those who prefer the armchair to the theatre-seat, who prefer to read scripts and imagine their own productions. That is all perfectly well, but it simply is not theatre. Those of us interested in theatre are concerned with the performed work, with the living art that playwrights, directors, designers, and actors create. When we go to the theatre, we go as members of actual audiences; and I will repeat still again that actual audiences obviously exist—indeed, the theatre is financially dependent upon them. But once we are in our seats, we begin the process of stepping out of ourselves, of putting ourselves in the role of the virtual audience at which the play is aimed. We begin to become the second persona[64] that the production implies. Very often, of course, we do not succeed, especially with performances that demand a great deal of us. In some cases, the play or the production is simply not worth the effort; in other cases, the pressures of the day interfere too much; and in yet others, we are simply not up to the task that faces us (and I remember with sadness certain performance occasions to which I could not rise). Thus, of all the actual audience members who see a play, only a small proportion may have been able to play the role of virtual audience. And, indeed, there may well be productions that have closed unseen by any member of a virtual audience. But despite all that, if we are to pursue our concern with the performed work, it must be the case that, when we succeed in playing our assigned role as virtual audience members, the work is somehow there for our inspection, not that it comes and goes depending on the whim or the reaction of this or that actual audience. Theatre *is* a living art, and every night the moment of truth comes when the play is re-formed before an audience, a re-forming that is accompanied by two paradoxes. First, the play is recreated before but not for that actual audience. And second, each performance makes manifest a theatrical form which is both ephemeral and permanent. Ephemeral in the sense that the performance ends, and the form is no longer there on stage. But permanent in the sense that the form, which existed in the human sensibility prior to the artwork, has now been given a local habitation, and as a result it will live in the minds of those of its viewers who could become a virtual audience. I can still remember Othello's first entrance in the 1946 Paul Robeson-José Ferrer-Uta Hagen production staged by Margaret Webster. A minor theatrical form was given life in that moment. Robeson entered, and it was as though a wall had moved onto the stage. One instinctively wanted to pull back. And I remember the major form that Robeson and Ferrer created, the biting, buzzing Iago and the slow, giant stateliness of Othello. Nearly forty years later, Christopher Plummer and James Earl Jones have created a remarkably different form, this one suffused with sexual and sensuous qualities. These two forms exist in my mind and in the minds of many others. In that sense, they are permanent. And that is to say that what every good production has to offer is a shaped form that is quite as objective and real—and long-lasting—as the form of a piece of music or dance. And like music and dance, the forms of theatre transcend particular audiences and audience responses.

It is the study of those forms of theatre that is the purpose of dramatic theory and criticism. In coming chapters, that study will range from the most specific to the most encompassing forms: from the use of example and argument in theatre, to the characters and the dramatic discourse of theatrical art, to the relationship between the implicit form of the script and the explicit form of the production, and, finally, to the major genres of theatre, tragedy and comedy.

Notes

[1]Margot Berthold, *A History of World Theatre*, translated by Edith Simmons (New York: Frederick Ungar Publishing Co., 1972), p. 14.

[2]J. L. Styan, *Drama, Stage and Audience* (London: Cambridge University Press, 1975), p. 224.

[3]Edwin Wilson, *The Theater Experience* (New York: McGraw-Hill Book Company, 1976), p. 13.

[4]Fred B. Millet and Gerald Eades Bentley, *The Art of the Drama* (New York: Appleton-Century-Crofts, 1963), p. 5.

[5]Kenneth Burke, *Counter-Statement* (Berkeley: University of California Press, 1968), p. 37.

[6]Walter Kerr, "We Call It 'Live' Theatre, But Is It?" *The New York Times*, 2 January 1972, cited in Wilson, *The Theater Experience*, p. 15.

[7] Jerzy Grotowski, "The Theatre's New Testament," cited in Bernard F. Dukore, *Dramatic Theory and Criticsm: Greeks to Grotowski* (New York: Holt, Rinehart and Winston, Inc., 1974), p. 982.

[8]*Brecht on Theatre*, edited and translated by John Willett (New York: Hill and Wang, 1964), p. 79.

[9] Oscar G. Brockett, *The Theatre: An Introduction*, third edition (New York: Holt, Rinehart and Winston, Inc., 1974), p. 25.

[10]Brander Matthews, *A Study of the Drama* (Boston: Houghton Mifflin Company, 1910), p. 87.

[11]Millet and Bentley, p. 5.

[12]Wilson, p. 16.

[13]Elmer Rice, *The Living Theatre* (New York: Harper and Brothers, 1959), p. 269.

[14]Aristotle *Poetics* 6. 1449b27-28. The quotation is from the Butcher translation. All future English quotations from the *Poetics* are taken from this source.

[15] Thorton Wilder, "Some Thoughts on Playwrighting," Dukore, p. 890.

[16]Rice, p. 270.

[17]Anita Block, *The Changing World in Plays and Theatre* (Boston: Little, Brown and Company, 1939, reprinted by Da Capo Press, New York, 1971), pp. 3, 4.

[18] Thelma Altshuler and Richard Paul Janaro, *Responses to Drama: An Introduction to Plays and Movies* (Boston: Houghton Mifflin Company, 1967), p. 12.

[19] Matthews, p. 78.

[20]Reference is made to these figures in Patti Peete Gillespie, "The Performing Audience," *The Southern Speech Communication Journal*, 46, 2 (Winter 1981), pp. 134-135. This article, together with my "The Theatre Audience: An Abstraction," appeared in the above source in a debate format, the articles plus two rebuttals. Readers are referred to Professor Gillespie's article and rebuttal for a full statement of the views I have summarized in this chapter.

[21]Gillespie, p. 135.

[22]Gillespie, p. 133.

[23]Gillespie, p. 133.

[24]Kerr, in Wilson, p. 15.

[25]Raymond Raver and Paul Anrieu, *Le Spectateur au Théâtre* (Brussels: *Institut de Sociologie de l'Université* de Bruxelles, 1964), p. 11. I borrow this example from Professor Gillespie.

[26]Brockett, p. 24.

[27]Tyrone Guthrie, "So Long as the Theatre Can Do Miracles," in *Edge of Darkness*, edited by Ned E. Hoopes and Richard Peck (New York: Dell Publishing Co., Inc., 1966), pp. 158, 163.

[28]Richard F. Shepard, "A New Portrait of the Theatregoer," *The New York Times*, 16 March 1980, Section D, p. 1.

[29]*The New York Cultural Consumer*, conducted for the American Council for the Arts in Education, Inc., with support from the New York State Council on the Arts, by National Research Center of the Arts, Inc., an affiliate of Louis Harris and Associates, Inc., 1976, pp. 10, 13, 16, 19. (Publication available from Publishing Center for Cultural Resources, 27 W. 53rd St., New York City 10019.)

[30]National Endowment for the Arts, Report 14, *Audience Development: An examination of selected analysis and prediction techniques applied to symphony and theatre attendance in four southern cities*, January 1981, p. 15.

[31] National Endowment for the Arts, Report 9, *Audience Studies of the Performing Arts and Museums: A Critical Review*, November 1978, p. 33. See especially pp. 75-102 for a rare bibliography of audience studies.

[32]William Gourd, "Cognitive Complexity and Theatrical Information Processing: Audience Responses to Plays and Characters," *Communication Monographs*, 44, 2 (June 1977).

[33] David W. Addington, "Varieties of Audience Research: Some Prospects for the Future," *Educational Theatre Journal*, 26, 4 (December 1974).

[34] Judith B. Kase, Sue M. Sikes, and Charles D. Spielberger, "Emotional Reactions to Frightening and Neutral Scenes in Story Theatre," *Communication Monographs*, 45, 2 (June 1978).

[35]Anthony Mulac and Mary Jo Rudd, "Effects of Selected American Regional Dialects Upon Regional Audience Members," *Communication Monographs*, 44, 3 (August 1977).

[36] For further items on the nature of the theatre audience, items which in general support these two points, see "Bibliography of Empirical Research in Theatre," *Empircal Research in Theatre*, 8 (Summer 1982), pp. 85-112.

[37] Moira Hodgson, "Makarov Stages A New 'Bayadère,' " *The New York Times*, 18 May 1980, Section D, p. 1.

[38] Anna Kisselgoff, "Ballet Theatre: New 'Bayadère,' " *The New York Times*, 23 May 1980, Section C, p. 16.

[39]Anna Kisselgoff, "Ballet: 'La Bayadère' With 2 New Male Leads," *The New York Times*, 26 May 1980, Section C, p. 14.

[40]See her "Ballet: 'Swan Lake' With Miss Thesmar," *The New York Times*, 29 May 1980, Section C, p. 16; also "Tudor's Tragic Masterpiece," *The New York Times*, 29 May 1980, Section C, p. 16; also "Tudor's Tragic Masterpiece," *The New York Times*, 1 June 1980, Section 2, p. 8; also "Dance: Godunov as Limon's Moor," *The New York Times*, 2 June 1980, section C, p. 18.

[41]Harold C. Schonberg, " 'Program' Versus 'Absolute'—The Debate Surfaces Again," *The New York Times*, 23 March 1980, Section D, p. 23.

[42]Harold C. Schonberg, "Schubert's Problem Operas," *The New York Times*, 25 May 1980, Section D, p. 19.

[43]John Rockwell, "Avant-Garde: Behrman and Lewis," *The New York Times*, 26 May 1980, Section C, p. 16.

[44]Harold C. Schonberg, "Why Isn't A Musical Comedy An Opera?" *The New York Times*, 25 November 1979, Section D, p. 1. Of course, Schonberg might have noted that if that was all there was to it, all musical comedies would be successes. But there is no *one* audience to adjust to; this audience may approve, that one may not.

[45]John Rockwell, "Today's Blank Art Explores the Space Behind the Obvious," *The New York Times*, 17 July 1977, Section D, p. 1.

[46]Rockwell, "Today's Blank Art Explores the Space Behind the Obvious," p. 1.

[47]Kisselgoff, "Ballet Theatre: New 'Bayadère.' "

[48]NEA Report # 9, p. 21.

[49]*The New York Cultural Consumer*, p. 239.

[50]See Gillespie, pp. 132-133.

[51]David P. Young, *Something of Great Constancy: The Art of "A Midsummer Night's Dream"* (New Haven: Yale University Press, 1966), pp. 15-16.

[52]Don Geiger, *The Sound, Sense and Performance of Literature* (Chicago: Scott Foresman and Company, 1963), p. 77.

[53]Northrop Frye, *The Anatomy of Criticism* (New York: Atheneum, 1967), pp. 4-5.

[54]Constantin Stanislavski, *Stanislavski Legacy: A Collection of Comments on a Variety of Aspects of an Actor's Art and Life*, editor and translator, Elizabeth Hapgood Reynolds, revised and expanded edition (New York: Theatre Arts Books, 1968), p. 134.

[55]S. H. Butcher, *Aristotle's Theory of Poetry and Fine Art* (New York: Dover Publications, Inc., 1951), pp. 207-208.)

[56]Butcher, p. 209.

[57]Butcher, pp. 210-211.

[58]Butcher, pp. 212-214.

[59]Gerald F. Else, *Aristotle's Poetics: The Argument* (Cambridge: Harvard University Press, Published in Cooperation with the State University of Iowa, 1967), p. 439.

[60]See Oscar G. Brockett and Robert R. Findlay, *Century of Innovation: A History of European and American Theatre and Drama Since 1870* (Englewood Cliffs, N.J.: Prentice-Hall, Inc., 1973), pp. 743-744.

[61]*The New York Times*, 6 June 1979, p. 16.

[62]*The New York Times*, 24 June 1979.

[63]*The New York Times*, 6 June 1979.

[64]Another example of such weakening is described in *The New York Times*, 23 August 1979, Section C, p. 14. Of a production of *As You Like It*, at the Long Beach, California Theatre Festival, the director claimed that the staging "was too sophisticated for the audience," but when one reads that "the rustics had rural American accents, Touchstone was a circus clown, and both dukes were played by actors who were nearly 7 feet tall and obviously chosen for their height rather than their acting abilities," one has one's doubts.

[64]Theatre people will find rewarding Edwin Black's "The Second Persona," *Quarterly Journal of Speech*, 56, 2 (April 1970). Black is concerned with the *personae* implied by rhetorical acts, but his argument, *mutatis mutandis*, can be applied most profitably to the productions of plays. See also Walker Gibson, "Authors, Speakers, Readers and Mock Readers," *College English*, 11 (1950.)

Chapter II

The Performers and the Performance

If it comes as something of a surprise to theatre people to find that the present day view of the theatre audience is not derived from the *Poetics*, it may be even more surprising to realize that that concept of the audience comes from the *Rhetoric*. Not from the work in which Aristotle discussed tragedy, but from the treatise on political, forensic, and ceremonial oratory. It is in the *Rhetoric* that one finds detailed treatments of the speaker-speech-audience model of communication. Change "speaker" to "performer" and "speech" to "performance," and you have the current view of the theatrical event, one in which performers are said to communicate with and to affect audience members. This view is strikingly similar to sections of the *Rhetoric:*

> Of the modes of persuasion furnished by the spoken word there are three kinds. The first kind depends on the personal character of the speaker; the second on putting the audience into a certain frame of mind; the third on the proof, or apparent proof, provided by the words of the speech itself.[1]

And as to the importance of the audience, the *Rhetoric* is quite clear:

> For of the three elements in speech-making—speaker, subject, and person addressed—it is the last one, the hearer, that determines the speech's end and object.[2]

In the *Poetics*, the idea of addressing the audience directly (a notion common to the *Rhetoric*) is absent, and, indeed, the audience itself is almost unmentioned (there are but three references to the audience in the entire work[3]). Nothing Aristotle says about tragedy is remotely comparable to Book I, Chapter 3 of the *Rhetoric*, with its definition of types of persuasion based on the types of audiences addressed; and, in fact, in Chapter 13 of the *Poetics*, Aristotle condemns tragedies that cater to spectators.

Now, having argued that the audience element of Aristotle's speech-speaker-audience model is unsatisfactory as a concept for dramatic theory and criticism, I want to turn to the remaining elements, speech and speaker, i.e., performer and performance.

The Speaker (The Performer)

The characters of a play are, perhaps, its most obvious formal elements, the most prominent of the devices created by and in the work. I have already argued that performances are aimed at virtual and not actual audiences; now I shall claim that those who address these virtual audiences are virtual and not actual speakers.

This is a perfectly simple matter, for in the theater it is not Shakespeare or Sir Laurence Olivier to whom one attends directly, but Hamlet; not Miller or Lee J. Cobb, but Willy Loman; not Anouilh or Julie Harris, but Joan of Arc. It is not the playwrights or the actors who are the immediate sources of dramatic discourse, but the characters they have created. At least, that is the case if the work is of even minimal quality; to attend to what actors *qua actors* are doing is ordinarily a sign that one is present at a personality display of some sort, not a work of theatre art. This is all obvious enough, but I shall do more in the way of systematic explanation later in this chapter.

Theatre, then, is a form in which the speaker, as one has known that being in Aristotle's *Rhetoric*, disappears. That is, there are actual speakers (the author and the actors), but they place themselves beyond our reach, and it is the virtual speakers, the characters, who address or pretend to address us.[4] These virtual speakers are not limited to theatre, for they are found, in varying degrees of clarity, in literature; but theatre is the only art in which they are openly and fully and physically enacted. Further, theatre is the only art in which actual speakers who are physically present pretend to be other than themselves and make no secret of that pretense. In rhetorical events such as public speeches, there may be a good deal of pretense, but usually the pretense is that there is no pretense.

Formally, theatre begins when virtual speakers take over from and overshadow actual speakers.

The Speech (The Performance)

Even if playscripts were never performed, one might regard them as formally distinct from, say, political speeches. The presence of the imaginary beings we call characters is, as I say, the most obvious formal element, but there are others. For instance, despite the limitations of Aristotelian theory, it is surprising to realize just how important the elements of Recognition and Reversal are in many, many plays. But theatre is not simply a group of playscripts, of course. Theatre is made up of texts-in-performance, and there are major formal differences between the work on the page and that same work on the stage.

On the most fundamental level of form, theatre is an utterly concrete and specific art. The one thing that is forever impossible (at least without incurring risks which I shall describe shortly) for actors, designers, and directors is the use of generalities. What one sees on stage is always some particular actor, and what that actor does is always to move and speak in some particular way. Designers never work simply with red or blue, but always with some specific shade of red or blue, never with large, rectangular flats, but always with flats of specific dimensions. In the playscript, one may see lines that one imagines as uttered angrily or sadly or gleefully, but in performance one always hears those lines spoken with one certain degree of anger or kind of sadness or sort of glee. Elements such as setting, movement, and tempo that are present only implicitly in the script are made manifest in the production of that script and become absolutely explicit. In the production, such elements are concrete examples of color, movement, volume, etc.; they are actual instances in which attitudes and emotions are enacted and, thereby, given immediacy. In brief, the theatre is an art form that deals always with particular cases, with *examples;* examples of melancholy, of changing tempos, of fading light, or what have you.

The point is not usually put in quite this manner, but it is essentially the same as the conventional claim that action or enactment is the core of dramatic form. From Aristotle to the present, theorists have agreed on this issue. Aristotle begins his definition of tragedy by saying that it is the imitation of an *action*,[5] and the key term "imitation" (*mimesis*) is more properly understood as *reenactment* rather than some sort of copying.[6] Butcher comments, "In the drama the characters are not described, they enact their own story and so reveal themselves."[4] Langer says the primary abstraction of drama is the *act*.[8] Jerzy Grotowski describes the core of theatre as the *action* of penetration and exposure on the part of the actor.[9] This consistent emphasis on action, on enactment brings forth, at least by implication, an opposing process, that of argument or assertion. In the theatre, it is never enough to argue or assert; characters come into existence via action or enactment. And in enactment, examples are created.

Of course, the idea of the artwork as example is not particularly new. Theorists such as Clive Bell and Edward Bullough have talked of the ways in which art is other than its surroundings, in which art does not function instrumentally, but simply is.[10] But while those views are similar to the notion I am proposing, they say nothing specific about the theatre and very little about the example as a formal device; further, they make no comment on those techniques the theatre cannot use or can use only in limited ways, and these are issues of considerable importance for the theatre.

Theatre centers on enactment or example that is overt, concrete, and explicit, and the example as a formal element brings with it great force. The primary effect of the example is the implication that something *is;*

examples have an extraordinary power of immediacy, for they imply the existence, the sheer objective fact of this or that person or thing or event. When Willy Loman speaks to his wife and his sons, we are not confronted with logical arguments about a defeated seeker after success in a changing society; we are faced with an example of that defeat that very powerfully is. *A Touch of the Poet* sets forth no argument about the inability to accept reality; it offers the example of Con Melody. When Mother Courage trudges off to another battlefield at the end of the play, we are not given a propositional argument about the devasting effect of the profit motive; we are presented with an example of that devastation, the sheer fact of which carries great force.

Characters in action are the essence of theatre, and these characters and their actions constitute examples that make up a form of considerable power. But of course, we are not used to thinking of examples in this fashion. We are used to examples as they appear in political speeches, sociological treatises, etc., where they are used to support some general statement or are derived from such a statement.

Examples so used are part of discursive form, part of argument. By contrast, the examples that are the core of theatre and that come into full existence in production are not ordinarily part of discursive form, i.e., they do not commonly occur in the reasoned move from premises to conclusions. In the theatre, one is not given a general statement or proposition and then provided with examples to support it, nor do those examples lead inferentially to such general statements. The examples of theatre do not serve a discursive purpose; instead, they imply that something is, that something exists and exits in the fictive world of the play, not the actual world of the audience. The value of the examples of theatre is not that they support general statements, but that they permit audience-members to project themselves into the characters (or introject the characters into themselves). In other words, examples provide the basis for identification, which is the primary response of the (virtual) audience.[11] The theatrical event is enacted via examples, and when it is enacted well, it is not because the examples serve some discursive end, but because they are gracefully selected, arranged, and presented.

Theatre and Argument. I have arrived at a point at which, to sustain my claim, I must differentiate very clearly between "argument" and "persuasion." "Argument" I use in the traditional sense of reasoning from premises to conclusions, not merely in the sense of dispute or controversy. Any matter put discursively is argument. Thus, it is not only the syllogism, but any process of formally laying down premises, providing data or evidence, and drawing conclusions, no matter how circuitous or indirect, that is argument. This essay is an argument; so are most theoretical works on the nature of theatre and most newspaper editorials. (One may note in passing that arguments are objective in the sense that they do not require an audience response in order to be considered arguments.)

"Persuasion" is a far broader term. It includes argument, when particular arguments are used as formal devices; it also includes all the means by which theatrical art works its effects, all the possible formal devices available to theatre. Antony's funeral oration in *Julius Caesar* is an interesting persuasive act (for both the Roman audience and the virtual audience to which any particular performance of the play is presented[12]), but it can hardly be called an argument. Antony's plays on words, his sarcasm, and the emotional appeals involving Caesar's cloak and his mutilated body do not qualify as reasoned progressions from premises to conclusions.

The theatre can always persuade, but it can argue only in a very limited fashion. For example, in *Amadeus* Mozart is shown suffering under the unjust deprivations forced on him by Salieri and under the agonizing drive of his own talent; this formal device offers no argument, yet makes Mozart the compelling center of attention. In *The Elephant Man*, John Merrick is mocked, ridiculed, finally treated decently, but always regarded as a medical oddity, a freak, or a plaything of society (except by Mrs. Kendal); and this technique, plus Merrick's almost unbelievable will to live as a human being, makes him the focus of the play. Neither of the last two plays presents an argument about its central character, but each is filled with persuasive devices that make us see the character in a certain light. (As is the case with arguments, these persuasive devices are objective in that they do not require the reaction of audiences to exist.)

Having distinguished between argument and persuasion in this fashion, the question remains as to whether argument as such is possible at all in theatre. This issue is most frequently raised in regard to literature, but the claims made are entirely applicable to theatre. The strongest view against the possibility of argument goes something like this: literary or theatrical works may persuade (in a sense), but they do not argue; and if they persuade, it is in an intuitive and not a reasoned manner; the theatre deals in images rather than discursive form, and it engages the feelings of the audience rather than ignoring those feelings, as philosophic argument does; in argument, principles and concepts are used in obedience to the law of contradiction, whereas the ambiguities and paradoxes of the theatre make the law of contradiction an enemy; finally, argument cannot occur in the theatre simply because truth claims cannot be made by fictional characters.[13]

The above view denies the possibility of argument outright, but there is a more complex approach that is possible. Stephen Ross holds that a literary or theatrical work sometimes "*displays* philosophical positions"; in other instances, philosophical positions "are constructed in such a way as virtually to make a case for the view presented."[14] Ross describes various works that display philosophical positions, including Camus' *The Stranger*, Tolstoi's *Anna Karenina*, and William Golding's *Lord of the Flies*. To illustrate the working out of philosophical claims and the justification of those claims in an artwork, he turns to Ugo Betti's *The Queen and the Rebels*, a play about an empty, despairing woman who helps a queen escape by pretending to be queen herself and then finds that she cannot stop pretending, that she wants to be queenlike, even though it means her death. It is Ross's position that, "in revealing that such possibilities are the pinnacle of human potentiality, the play cannot but be moral to the fullest extent,"[15] and he says that the play, in being moral, makes a moral claim on its audiences:

> What grounds exist for demanding of an individual that he place moral demands higher than self-interest? Betti simply demonstrates, through the medium of art, that moral heroism can be true self-interest, far more than mere self-preservation.... It is difficult to imagine what kind of evidence would be relevant if this is not.... Presented in such compelling form, it constitutes justification for the claim that the reader too, or other men, should act in like manner and that they will have similar experiences.... If the point of the play were only to show us *one* woman undergoing *her* special experiences, the level of identification, the rapport between audience and actress and the power of the play would be lost. It is only as moral, both with a thesis and with a defense of that thesis in its very form and arrangement, that *The Queen and the Rebels* is a wonderful play.[16]

However, Ross is careful to admit and to emphasize:

> If an argument exists to support Betti's thesis, it is that other men have found it immediately and directly rewarding to act nobly rather than to humble themselves out of fear. But such an argument must also include evidence to show that those other men are not unique, that they are not superior beings different from other men. Betti, precisely by presenting Argia in such humble form at the beginning and showing how events could render her both heroic and pleased to be so, presents precisely this argument in both its forms. However, since it is not given explicitly in discursive language, with premises and conclusion, it may not be useful to call it an "argument." Furthermore, the presentation is made in the realm of possibilities, which renders it rather different from a typical argument.[17]

But having recognized as much, Ross nevertheless concludes:

If we grant the credibility of Argia's portrayal, her resemblance to people that we know, to ourselves if we need not strain too far to understand and appreciate her, then we are in effect granting Betti's *premise*: that her fortunes and experiences are indeed relevant to our own. Therefore his conclusion follows, virtually as if argued for; though it follows from the manner of presentation, not from the logical arguments set forth in propositional form.[18]

Neither of these views, that theatre is incapable of argument and that theatre is very like argument in some cases, is satisfactory. (I know of no one who seriously claims that theatre presents arguments in syllogistic form.[19]) Argument does, indeed, occur in theatre, but it occurs in a particular form and in a sharply limited fashion. As for Ross, he attempts to have it both ways: he speaks of "argument," "thesis," "premise," etc., but he admits that Betti's play does not provide an argument in discursive terms, that it does not offer premises and conclusion. If one inspects the playscript closely, one will find that no premise is advanced, no evidence is supplied (that Argia is like the rest of us), and no conclusion is drawn. What the play does is to offer the *example* of Argia acting in a certain way in a certain situation. True, a viewer or reader may take the example Betti provides and build an argument around it, as Ross has, but that argument is not in the play.[20] In sum, Ross's concept of argument in this and similar plays is unsatisfactory for at least four reasons. First, if the example in Betti's play is enough to qualify as argument, all plays become arguments, for all plays present examples of characters in given situations. Second, Ross limits himself to philosophical arguments, and plays can make arguments about political or social or military or even scientific issues. Third, all of Ross's claims can be granted by simply saying that a theatrical work is persuasive, and this avoids the difficulties that Ross's position leads to. And fourth, there are plays that present clearly recognizable arguments, not the tenuous and vaguely argument-like process that Ross describes in the Betti play. *Major Barbara* is an instance of such a play; there is an unmistakable and very diverting argument conducted between Undershaft, Cusins, and Barbara, an argument about the nature of humanity and industrial societies. And at many points that argument is formally explicit; in Act III, Undershaft voices the premise that money saves souls, and he supports that premise by showing that his workers are morally better off than those who sought help in Barbara's Salvation Army shelter.

The fact that explicit arguments occur in plays is not only evidence that weakens Ross's position, it is a direct denial of the claim that argument cannot exist in the theatre. Instances supporting the view that argument *does* exist come to mind easily. *Inherit the Wind* is a play in which an argument, a clear discursive argument is conducted between the thinly disguised William Jennings Bryan and Clarence Darrow characters. The fictional Bryan relies on the Bible as authority, and the Darrow character depends heavily on logical reasoning. The argument is unmistakable, and yet the strength of the play lies in the dramatic confrontation between the two figures, not in the power or scope of the argument presented. In fact, looked at purely as argument, the play is quite frail: the strengths and weaknesses of the Bible as an authoritative source are never adequately explored, and the scientific views of evolution are never set forth in any detail. Anouilh's *Antigone* is a similar case: the clash between Antigone and Creon involves more than example, for Creon justifies his refusal to allow Polynices to be buried on the basis of political need. Antigone's position, however, is that she must bury Polynices, not for religious reasons, not for political reasons, but simply for herself. Hence, regarded strictly as argument, the play is weak; its chief interest lies in the contest of wills between Antigone and Creon, not in the quality of the arguments they present. Even a play as frivolous as *The Madwoman of Chaillot* makes an argument against the evils of capitalism, though it is not the argument but the triumphantly eccentric characters that are the strength of the play. Other plays of this sort might be mentioned,[21] but upon close inspection they turn out to be interesting or powerful as dramatic forms, not as propositional arguments. These plays depend upon the example as their primary formal device and while they may go beyond example to argument, the arguments created are secondary or even incidental in importance and often of poor quality. Of course, it is not as arguments that these plays are perceived, and their discursive weaknesses are not considered to be faults in the dramatic structures.

But there are still other plays in which one finds arguments that are neither incidental to the work nor poorly structured, and an examination of such plays is informative. Shaw's works can lead one to the sort of play I have in mind. His *Major Barbara* I have already referred to as a dramatic form within which arguments are made, though they are of secondary importance. But *Man and Superman* is another matter; here the discursive argument is not incidental to the dramatic action, but for large sections of the play, e.g., the Act III debate between Don Juan and The Devil, *is* the dramatic action. As a result, the play can seem "talky" and can be difficult to stage; parts of it are very like attempting to stage a piece of so-called nondramatic literature, for the concrete examples essential to actor, designer, and director are sometimes implied only vaguely by the script. Indeed, example is not always the central formal device in this play, and when it is not, the theatre of example moves toward the theatre of argument. But Shaw avoids crossing the boundary (or at least he crosses it with a certain sneaky wit), and *Man and Superman* lies, I would say, at the approximate dividing line between the theatre of example and the theatre of argument. When one goes further beyond this boundary, one finds didactic and propaganda plays such as the "living newspapers," Odets' *Waiting for Lefty* and *Awake and Sing!*, John Howard Lawson's *Loud Speaker* and *Marching Song*, Trevor Griffith's *The Party*, many (or all) of Brecht's *Lehrstucke*, Dumas *fils' Le Fils Naturel*, Howard Fast's *Thirty Pieces of Silver*, The Living Theatre's *Paradise Now*, and occasional experimental works of the 1960s and 1970s. Most of these plays go well beyond *Man and Superman*, for they are works in which argument is often or always the principal formal device employed. Though they differ in various ways, these plays are similar in that, while they may have importance as social and historical documents, they are of limited value as theatre. The displacement of example and enactment by assertion and argument means that the theatrical work is diminished, for argument *qua* argument is not the stuff of theatre. (One is reminded of Thorton Wilder's statement: "Many attempts have been made to present Plato's dialogues, Gobineau's fine series of dialogues, *La Renaissance*, and the *Imaginary Conversations* of Landor; but without success....An action is required and an action that is more than a mere progress in argumentation and debate."[22]) Because plays such as those mentioned are made up largely of argument, the characters must spend their time in discursive rather than dramatic action; hence, they do not vividly establish themselves via enactment; and what results are sociological treatises, political statements, or calls to social action. These sociological or political tracts are presented in dramatic form, quite as philosophical arguments can be presented in dramatic form; in fact, Ross himself says, "Where careful and detailed analysis is offered, however literarily, which leads to very specific conclusions, we tend to consider the work primarily philosophical, rather than artistic—as in the Platonic dialogues."[23] Just as those philosophical arguments are valued primarily as philosophy, the didactic works I am describing are valued primarily as social or political statements (or as part of theatre history). The claim I make here, though not widely echoed, can be supported by the many standard sources that either cite the historical value of these plays, while saying little about their artistic merit, or caution against use of explicit argument by playwrights;[24] support is also provided by the relatively infrequent productions given these works.

My position is that argument occurs in the theatre, and occurs quite frequently, but that theatrical works are never primarily argumentative in nature; that is, when the arguments presented are well-made and important enough to stand on their own, the work of theatre art is lessened. The theoretical explanation of this useful but limited role of argument in the theatre has been provided by Susanne Langer. To summarize her discussions of "discursive" and "presentational" form, discursive form proceeds analytically in the process of reasoning from premises to conclusions; that is, discursive form occurs in language, and the parts of language that go to make up an argument are meaningful in their own right; such parts may be, and are, studied and evaluated as separate items. By contrast, a work of theatre art (indeed, any artwork) is synthetic in that it is meaningful only as a whole; and the elements that comprise the work draw their meaning from the fact that they are part of the whole; while those elements may have certain values or meanings when considered in isolation, when they are *assimilated* into the artwork, they lose the earlier values and become formal elements of that work.[25] Just so do arguments and fragments of argument occur in theatre; they are assimilated into the theatrical form and are used for dramatic and not discursive ends. (This is, as I say, a summary of Langer's concepts. Her distinctions between discursive and presentational form are quite complex, and misreadings of her claims are extraordinarily easy. Langer's work is, in my judgment, of major importance to theatre scholars, but in order to avoid retarding my own argument unduly at this point, I have placed the discussion of Langer's concepts of the two forms in Appendix I.)

Presentational form can be found even in the text, for the characters and their enactments are outside discursive form. But it is with the production that nondiscursive form is most clearly seen. As produced, a play consists of various physical materials, human bodies and voices, colors, shapes, sounds, tempi, etc., plus words. Only the last of these elements is (sometimes, by no means always) discursive in nature. Theatre, *all* theatre, is overwhelmingly presentational in form. One may distinguish between action plays and talk plays, but a moment's thought shows that the talkiest play to be found is replete with actors' bodies and movements, a setting of some sort (even if only a bare stage), lighting, costumes (even if only street dress), and so forth. In other words, theatre can never be primarily discursive in nature, for the large number of nonverbal and nondiscursive elements make that an impossibility. *Unless,* of course, the characters turn from enactment to argument, and then the over-all presentational form weakens, elements such as setting and costume lose their dramatic function and become insignificant, and the element of argument, instead of being assimilated into a theatrical form, becomes itself the ruling form.

Theatre, then, is a limited art form. I mentioned earlier that the example as a formal device carries great force. It does, but it is also subject to severe limitations. Because theatre depends on the example and can use argument only in a secondary manner, it is not capable of treating complex ethical issues, or of analyzing intricate political situations, or of investigating the moral problems of freedom, evil, etc. Such topics require discursive treatment, and the theatre cannot spin out the long, taut arguments that would be needed to handle them. This limitation on what the theatre can do also has its roots in Aristotle: Else notes, "There is in fact not a word in the *Poetics* about the ultimate 'secrets of life,' about why mankind should suffer or be happy, about Fate, or man's relation to God, or any such metaphysical matter."[26] It was for philosophy to argue such matters, not for the theatre, according to the Greeks. And the point remains today. The theatre cannot unravel the causes of social unrest, or trace the decline of the family in the United States, or explicate the relationship between heredity and environment. It can argue such issues, but only within very sharp limits, and its arguments are always simple, always relatively unimportant, and often poor in quality. As a result, the theatre cannot satisfactorily explain the nature of tyranny or the basis of feminism; what it can do is offer us the examples of Creon and Nora Helmer.

And now, in claiming that the use of argument in theatre is tightly restricted, I have raised another issue, that of language and its importance to the performed work.

Theatre and Language. Discursive form means the process of reasoning from premises to conclusion; this process takes place in language, but discursive form is *not* to be equated with language for the simple reason that in many instances language presents no argument at all. Neither in lyric poetry nor in works that are purely descriptive are there arguments. Nor in *The Queen and the Rebels* or *Waiting for Godot* or many, many other plays is there an argument. But to say that discursive form is absent from some plays and must be of no more than secondary importance in others, is to say, not nothing, but far too little about the function of language. Put simply, language is fundamental to theatre; the theatre could not exist without it.[27] There are three kinds of evidence that support this claim. First, if one starts with the staged work and begins to abstract from that work, the process of abstraction will inevitably end with the playscript. That is, there are many items that can be deliberately abstracted from the produced work, the lighting, make-up, etc.; but if one goes about the process of abstracting in the usual fashion, retaining to the end those items that most directly imply the existence of *other* important theatrical elements, one will finish with the script. One does not drop out the script in favor of, say, the actors, because the sheer fact of actors does not imply the dialogue of the play, whereas the dialogue does imply the characters who are impersonated by actors. The fact that the process of abstraction concludes with the script means that only the script allows a play to be staged and then repeated night after night; the most complete description imaginable of the sets, lighting, or costumes would not permit the realization of the performed work if the script were absent, while scripts that make no direct mention of other elements do lead to full theatrical productions. Second, if one begins at the logical beginning, one starts with the script.[28] Chronologically one may begin anywhere, with a gesture, a piece of music, a set, or any one of a multitude of items that is psychologically provocative. But the script is the only logical beginning in the sense that it is only the script that can guide one to the remaining elements with any surety at all. One may start with a lighting design or with costumes and find it impossible to reach a fully orchestrated theatrical production. But the script is capable of functioning as a *score*; it is the nucleus that begins the complete work and that guides one, in at least a general sense, to that complete work. The script has this power because it alone is a symbol system. One may properly call specific colors, or movements, or shapes symbols, but they are not symbol *systems*. And the script alone provides the symbol system that is capable of ordering the many nonverbal and nondiscursive items that make up the theatrical work and, thereby, giving it form and coherence. Third, of the various elements that contribute to the full theatrical work, only the script has the status of an artwork in its own right. It is, I would argue, an incomplete work, but it is, nonetheless, the case that one reads plays to one's profit and pleasure. To do so, of course, one must read the script as a score, imagining, not specific actors and line-readings, but formal and structural elements of performance, much as a musician reads a musical score. Nothing outside the script, not even such extravagant settings as those used in the New York productions of *Sweeney Todd, Cats,* or *K2* is artistically meaningful on its own.

For most of the twentieth century, the emphasis has been on the nonverbal elements of theatre.[29] Brecht, Artaud, and Grotowski have been the leaders in this movement. But Grotowski has now left the theatre for other means of experimentation,[30] Artaud produced no theatrical works of importance, and Brecht's plays, like all others, depend for their permanence and their performances on the scripts. Recently, a good many authors have commented on the importance of language in the theatre,[31] and thus my claim here is by no means radical.

Language is essential to theatre; indeed, for many the image most representative of theatre art is that of Aase, or Arkadina, or Dona Ana, or Antigone standing on the stage speaking to us. *Speaking* to us, badgering us, pleading with us, discoursing to us. And discourse it is, in a sense, but discourse that is an unformulable amalgam of verbal and nonverbal, discursive and nondiscursive elements. Not actual, but virtual discourse.

One might very sensibly ask what it is that holds all this together.

Have I simply traded the old, discredited notion of theatre as a combination of literature, architecture, painting, etc., for a new notion of theatre as a combination of different items? No, for there is, I think, a strong theoretical basis on which to argue that theatre is a single, unified form.

Elias Schwartz, drawing on the work of Jacques Maritain, describes plays as consisting of signs, images, and symbols.[32] Signs are items conveying meaning; images are items that are formally like something else; and anything that is both sign and image is a symbol. The important next point is that *signs, images, and symbols can have direct and reverse functions*. Direct signs refer to objects or events, real or imaginary; reverse signs tell us about the user of the signs. In the theatre, these distinctions have great explanatory power. The words of a playscript are direct signs that tell us about human actions and feelings (though not necessarily the actions and feelings of actual persons); at the same time, those words are reverse signs that give us information about the characters using them. These two sign functions exist on the formal level of the script. But in the performed work, the facial movements, gestures, tones of voice, etc., of the actors are images (formally like other movements, gestures, etc.), and it is in the reverse function of these images that characters come to life on stage. Then, the play as a whole is a symbol (or series of symbols); it may have a direct function of considerable importance, as in the cases of *Abe Lincoln in Illinois, The Corn is Green* and *The Diary of Anne Frank*, all of which have biographical or historical meanings. But the more significant function of the play as a symbol is always a reverse function, one in which a fictive world is brought into being. The written words of the text may function as direct signs and images, but the spoken words of the performance function also as reverse signs and images; if there is a discursive element in the play, it is the product of direct signs and images, but, concurrently, the reverse function of those signs and images creates the presentational dimension of the work. Although both direct and reverse functions are involved in the verbal element of the play, it is the reverse functions that are far more important in creating the nonverbal elements, e.g., the characters, their movements, needs, and conflicts. In sum, the theoretical formulation is that the *same* signs, images, and symbols create, and create simultaneously, all the elements that make up the artwork and that this is possible because of the direct and reverse functions of those signs, images, and symbols, functions which create dramatic or virtual discourse.

The Performance vs. the Text

For some time now, I have been talking of this or that aspect of performance. But the fact of the theatrical matter is that there are two faces of performance, or at least it is convenient to consider them as two faces. Much of the richness and flexibility of theatre as an artform comes from the Janus-faced nature of performance, that is, from the fact that performance can work with or against the playscript. The most usual procedure is, of course, for the two elements, the two forms to be consonant, for the performance to be fitted to the text. But the relationship between the two is not always as simple as that. While the performance is usually subordinate to the text, on occasion the performance can be the controlling force, and there are many times when the performance is deliberately used to modify, to discount, even to mock the playscript.

Perhaps the most obvious instances of the deliberate clash between the two elements occur because of social attitudes that differ from those of the period of composition or initial performance of the play. For example, anti-Semitism and sexism are social evils that have received wide comment, and, as a result, it can be quite difficult to mount productions of *The Merchant of Venice* or *The Taming of the Shrew*. Protestations that those plays are not "really" sexist or anti-semitic are unavailing, for the text is quite clear on those matters. As a result, when those plays are staged, one may well witness a performance that alters the text, e.g., Shylock may be shown as one who is trapped by persons not nearly as "Christian" as the text asserts (and the text merely asserts their Christianity, it does not allow them to enact it), and Kate may be played as a bride who pretends to docility but who has some startling plans in mind for her oppressor.

Differences between the performance and the text are present, though perhaps less obvious, in the cases of plays produced first in one country, then in another. As of this writing, recent examples have included Pinter's *Betrayal*, Martin Sherman's *Bent*, Stoppard's *Night and Day*, and *The Real Thing*, Andrew Lloyd Webber's and Tim Rice's *Evita*, Hugh Leonard's *Da*, and David Rudkin's *Ashes*. These plays were first staged in London, then in New York, or vice versa, and in every case the second production differed noticeably from the first, partly because different casts were involved, but also because the directors aimed at different virtual audiences.[33] A particularly interesting case is D. L. Coburn's *The Gin Game*, played on Broadway by Jessica Tandy and Hume Cronyn and staged at the Mayakovsky Theatre in Moscow with, among other striking changes, an added prologue in which an actor portrays Coburn and tells the audience that he wrote the play after seeing Gogol's *Diary of a Madman*.[34] All these second productions differed from the first because of what I call here the second face of performance.

But, of course, it need not be simply a matter of changed social attitudes or different cultures. In New York, Joseph Papp's production of *Two Gentlemen from Verona* changed the period, the specific setting, much of the dialogue, and some of the characters of the play; Andrei Serban directed a highly stylized version of *The Cherry Orchard*; Joseph Chaikin emphasized the humor in Beckett's *Endgame*. Some plays have had almost unbelievably varied production histories, and *A Midsummer Night's Dream* is one of these. Mendelssohn wrote his overture for a famous 1827 Berlin production; a key staging was that of Harley Granville Barker in 1914, a staging in which stylized (for the time) sets formed the fairies' world and the fairies themselves were bronzed and made to move like puppets; Max Reinhardt's mid-1920s film version with Dick Powell as Lysander, Mickey Rooney as Puck, and James Cagney as Bottom was seen by millions; Joseph Papp's 1961 production permitted horseplay to overshadow the language and the poetry of the play; Peter Brook's 1970 production, another key one, had the stage enclosed by white walls, trapezes as perches for the actors, and circus-like coveralls for costumes; the Tyrone Guthrie in 1982 did a touring production in which all the fairies and all the mechanicals except for Bottom were eliminated and in which the play was treated as a 1930's movie fantasy with Titania played as a Jean Harlow type, Oberon as John Barrymore, and with Puck as a hotel bellboy—the setting, a resort island in the tropics. In these and a great many other cases, production values were used to alter the meaning of the text quite substantially, not because the play was crossing national boundaries or encountering new social values, but because the director was seeking new insights into the work. This is the trickiest business imaginable, and there is always danger in pitting one of the forms against the other. Novelty sought for its own sake may very well weaken, perhaps even degrade, the play. Indeed, of the first three productions mentioned above, the second one was probably the single success (in the sense of appealing to the best possible virtual audience). Further, there are cases in which deliberate conflict between the two forms should never be attempted; the Goodspeed Opera House in Connecticut has made a name for itself by observing this dictum, by reviving old musicals and usually producing them in a straightforward fashion, using production values that treat the material with respect and only rarely exaggerating or making fun of the text or music.

But regardless of the danger, it is because of the produced work that we can have new *Othellos* and *Medeas*. It is because productions have changed the values of the text that such works are re-formed in staging after staging. We have seen, in the middle two quarters of this century, the lyric Hamlet of Maurice Evans, the pure and formal Hamlet of John Gielgud, the heroic Hamlet of Laurence Olivier, the angry, snarling Hamlet of Nicol

Williamson, and a great many others, and we have seen them, not because the words of the script were changed, but because the meanings of those words were altered by new productions. It is when the productions are made to war wittily and with grace against the scripts that we have fresh, vibrant ways of staging that mass of plays that makes up the great, central tradition in theatre. Indeed, it is this second face of performance, the possibility of using this second form to comment on the form of the text, that is the equivalent of metaphor in theatre. Meaning in the theatre, as outside it, is contextually dependent. Every sign, image, and symbol of a play exists within two contexts, the one of the script, the other of the production; in general terms, these can be considered the verbal and nonverbal contexts. When one of these contexts is significantly and appropriately altered, there occurs the metaphorical shift that produces new meanings. It is idle foolery to claim that Olivier's cold, disdainful "Get thee to a nunnery" speech was made up of the *same* words in semantic terms as Williamson's hoarsely passionate speech as he caressed Ophelia.

It is the enormous importance of performance functioning in its two capacities that makes me consider its one form when it agrees with, strengthens, reenforces the text, and another form when it emends, alters, opposes the text. It is surely true that a great many, perhaps a large majority of the attempts to change the text with the values of the production fail, partially or wholly. As surely, it is these attempts that make possible a living theatre.

In the text, the formal devices (especially the characters) that will constitute the performed work are implicitly present. But in the production, those elements become the explicit examples that are the heart of theatre. No other art attains the strength, or the narrowness, of the theatre of example, for the force of its immediacy is counterbalanced by its inability to conduct careful and extended argument. In these two forms, language is essential, and unity is guaranteed by the simultaneous direct and reverse functions of signs, images, and symbols. Finally, theatre possesses the reflexive power that is the second face of performance, the ability to turn back on its own materials and to challenge or change them.[36]

Theatre: the extraordinary form in which virtual speakers direct virtual discourse to a virtual audience.

The Minor Forms/The Forms of Mind

At the end of the last chapter, I mentioned a minor form that had been created with Robeson's entrance in the 1946 Robeson/Ferrer *Othello*. Nearly everything I have discussed in this chapter can be considered a major form of theatre. The exception, of course, is the direct and reverse functions of signs, images, and symbols, functions which can include individual words, movements, facial expressions, and the like. But now I want to talk about a level of form that is even more fundamental than such signs.

Burke discusses form on various levels, the most basic of which he calls minor forms:[37]

> When analyzing a work of any length, we may find it bristling with minor or incidental forms—such as metaphor, paradox, disclosure, reversal, contraction, expansion, bathos, apostrophe, series, chiasmus—which can be discussed as formal events in themselves.[38]

These forms are at once properties of the artwork and forms of mind:

> Throughout the permutations of history, art has always appealed, by the changing individuations of changing subject-matter, to certain potentialities of appreciation which would seem to be inherent in the very germ-plasm of man, and which, since they are constant, we might call forms of the mind. These forms are the "potentiality for being interested in certain processes or arrangements," or the "feeling for such arrangements of subject-matter as produce crescendo, contrast, comparison, balance, repetition, disclosure, reversal, contraction, expansion, magnification, series, and so on."[39]

One has but to put the two lists side by side to see that the minor forms either are or are easily translated into the forms of mind. And the tie between the two is essential to Burke's claim that "the formal aspects of art appeal in that they exercise formal potentialities of the reader. They enable the mind to follow processes amenable to it."[40]

These forms are logically prior to any particular artwork. In the case of theatre, this is trivially true in the sense that (at least most of the time) the form of the produced work is implied in the script. It is more than trivially true in the sense that form as it appears in theatre is a reflection of the forms used by the mind. The formal properties of theatre art reveal to us the forms of mind; in other words, they disclose to the human mind the mind itself. As Burke emphasizes, "Though forms need not be prior to experience, they are certainly prior to the work of art exemplifying them;"[41] "they apply in art, since they apply outside of art."[42] Indeed,

> so far as the work of art is concerned they simply *are*: when one turns to the production or enjoyment of a work of art, a formal equipment is already present, and the effects of art are involved in its utilization. Such ultimate minor forms as contrast, comparison, metaphor, series, bathos, chiasmus, are based upon our modes of understanding anything; they are implicit in the processes of abstraction and generalization by which we think.[43]

(Note that in this third list Burke combines items from lists one and two and thereby makes even clearer the fact that the ultimate forms are the forms of mind.)

All this has a Platonic ring, of course, and Burke points out that there was much to be said for Plato's doctrine of pure forms:

> We need but take his universals out of heaven and situate them in the human mind (a process begun by Kant), making them not metaphysical, but psychological. Instead of divine forms, we now have "conditions of appeal."[44]

The list of the forms of mind is not complete, as Burke admits: "Such 'forms of the mind' might be listed at greater length. But I shall stop at the ones given, as I believe they illustrate to the extent of being a definition of my meaning."[45] The list is not complete, and my task now will be, not to complete it, but at least to add some items—items that will be immediately familiar to theatre people.

Entrances, Exits. Along with the list Burke provides, these very basic theatrical forms are, I believe, also forms of human understanding. I mean by those terms the entrances and exits, not necessarily of persons, but even of forces, or powers, or imaginary entities. And notice that entrance and exit probably imply a locale or setting of some specificity; it is sensible to say she entered the courtyard, or the valley, but may be odd to say she entered the world. Thus, two forms even more basic may be needed: *Appearance, Disappearance*, as when a person, or quality, or force comes into being or ceases to exist.

Beings. Certainly this form is needed. I use this term rather than "characters," for I want to include ghosts, faeries, dragons, who knows what. It seems to me that, given the essentially dramatic nature of the human mind, one of the first things we do in thinking, in perceiving the world around us is to people it, to create a cast of *dramatis personae*. Our anthropomorphizing bent allows us to use rocks, trees, clouds, abandoned houses, or what have you as personages, and our dreams, of course, throng with such creations.

And with the scene set even thus sparsely, the grammar of theatre begins to take over. If beings or forces can enter and exit, can appear and disappear, we must have these further forms: *Approach, Withdrawal*. Two persons or powers draw near to each other, or to a third person, or they withdraw. Then this: *Confrontation*. A certain kind of approach can result in the two opposing each other. And that means additional forms: *Superior, Inferior*. One being or element dominates, the other submits; one commands, the other obeys; or simply, one is stronger, the other weaker. And these: *Invitation, Acceptance, Rejection*. One is enticed, lured (by beauty, power, immortality), and one accepts or rejects. And unmistakably these: *Beginning, Ending.* Other arts deal with these forms, but nowhere can they be seen more clearly than in the curtain parting (or going up) and closing (or coming down). Certainly our structuring of the world is done in terms of beginnings and endings; as a matter of mind, we use these forms.

Finally, these two: *Identity, Consubstantiality.*[46] As something or someone has identity, it is identifiable, it is of its own substance, separate from others; as something or someone is consubstantial with another, it shares substance with that other. The characters presented to us on stage are clearly other than ourselves, but as we identify with them, project ourselves into them, we become one with them (or they with us). And as a matter of course, we see ourselves in the world around us, sometimes even in physical objects; or we see the world as other than, as alien to ourselves.

These forms seem to me to be peculiarly theatrical, not in the sense that they are found in no other art, but in the sense that they are seen most clearly and fully in theatre. And in the sense that they are dynamic forms; action is necessary to each of them. Having said that, I am prompted to look again at Burke's list(s), to see whether there are items there that have specifically theatrical meanings that should be stressed. *Reversal,* of course, is the obvious example. While lights coming up and then being dimmed out might be considered a kind of reversal, one wants to be very sure that the Aristotelian sense of the term is included. Which means that another form must be added: *Recognition.* Recognition in the most abstract sense: a setting or situation or event that was incomprehensible can suddenly be recognized, be understood for what it is; this in addition to the recognition of persons.

The list is not complete, but, like Burke, I am content to stop with these examples as illustrative of the importance of theatrical forms to the human mind. In the final chapter, I shall suggest that *A Midsummer Night's Dream* demonstrates the importance of certain of these forms in theatre art.

Notes

[1]Aristotle *Rhetoric* 1. 2. 1356al-4. The W. Rhys Roberts translation. All English language quotations are from this source.

[2]Aristotle *Rhetoric* 1. 3. 1358a37-b1.

[3]Aristotle *Poetics* 4. 1449a7-9; 13. 1453a45; 25. 1461b28-62a3.

[4]There are, of course, a few cases in which the attempt is made to avoid any actor-audience separation; the Living Theatre was, perhaps, the most obvious of these. See the description in Oscar G. Brockett and Robert R. Findlay, *Century of Innovation: A History of European and American Theatre and Drama Since 1870* (Englewood Cliffs, N.J.: Prentice Hall, Inc., 1973), pp. 740-745. For a representative comment, a negative comment, on the attempt to bridge the actor-audience gap, see J. L. Styan, *The Elements of Drama* (London: Cambridge University Press, 1963), pp. 231-255. And there have been attempts to avoid acting entirely; the Open Theatre was one such effort. See Brockett and Findlay, pp. 752-759.

[5]*Poetics* 6. 1449b22-24.

[6]Helmut Kuhn makes this point in "Aesthetics, History of," *Encyclopedia Britannica*, 1966. And Paul Hernadi says, "Few modern critics regard the world of a work as the 'imitation' of something external to itself. Indeed, the original connotations of the Greek word point to 'representation' as a better translation of *mimesis*." *Beyond Genre: New Directions in Literary Classification* (Ithaca: Cornell University Press, 1972), p. 83.

[7]S. H. Butcher, *Aristotle's Theory of Poetry and Fine Art* (New York: Dover Publications, Inc., 1951), p. 335.

[8]Susanne K. Langer, *Feeling and Form* (New York: Charles Scribner's Sons, 1953), ch. 17.

[9]Jerzy Grotowski, "The Theatre's New Testament," in *Dramatic Theory and Criticism*, p. 985.

[10]See Clive Bell, "Art as Significant Form: The Aesthetic Hypothesis" and Edward Bullough, " 'Psychical Distance' as a Factor in Art and an Aesthetic Principle," both in *Aesthetics: A Critical Anthology*, edited by George Dickie and Richard J. Sclafani (New York: St. Martin's Press, 1977); also, Langer, *Feeling and Form*, chs. 2-4.

[11]The audience response contains a rational or judgmental element, as I argued in the first chapter. But that is not to say that the audience builds discursive arguments out of the examples the theatre provides. This would require that the audience forage far afield from the work confronting them, as I shall show later in the chapter.

[12]See Kenneth Burke, "Antony in Behalf of the Play," *The Philosophy of Literary Form* (Berkeley: University of California Press, 1973), pp. 329-343.

[13]For statements on the possibility of argument in literature and drama, see Hugh Mercer Curtler, "Does Philosophy Need Literature?" *Philosophy and Literature*, 2, 1 (Spring 1978), pp. 110-115; "Philosophy Needs Literature," *Philosophy and Literature*, 1, 2 (Spring 1977), pp. 170-182; Charles Kauffman, "Poetic as Argument," *Quarterly Journal of Speech*, 67 4 (November 1981) and David Rod, "Judgment as an Element of Audience" Response in Aristotle's *Poetics The Theatre Annual*, xxxvi, 1981. My own belief is that to treat seriously the notion that truth claims cannot be made by fictional characters plunges one into all sorts of problems. For one thing, it is by no means easy to tell when an author is using a fictional character. Is Plato's "Socrates" the historical being or a fiction of Plato's creation? Certainly there are discrepancies between the dialogues that make it difficult to regard Socrates as based on straightforward historical fact. And is it appropriate to declare that an author cannot deliberately put an argument, truth claims and all, in the mouth of a character? That position would appear to be enmeshed in all sorts of intentional fallacies. Finally, if one reads an argument, is it the case that one cannot tell whether or not truth claims are made unless one knows that the argument was written by an author speaking in her or his own person? If so, then arguments have no objective status, a view that seems most difficult to uphold.

[14]Stephen D. Ross, *Literature & Philosophy* (New York: Appleton-Century-Crofts, 1969), pp. 3, 6-7.

[15]Ross, p. 37.

[16]Ross, pp. 37-38.

[17]Ross, pp. 39-40.

[18]Ross, p. 41.

[19]The closest thing to this may be Joseph N. Calarco, "Tragedy as Demonstration," *Educational Theatre Journal*, 18, 2 (May 1966), 271-274. Calarco argues that *Oedipus Tyrannus*, for instance, is made up of a premise, middle, and conclusion and is, therefore, like a giant syllogism. Unfortunately, Calarco does not define these terms, and the middle, he says, is simply the play.

[20]It may be tempting to think that Ross is referring to an enthymeme or an enthymeme-like structure, one in which the audience supplies a missing premise. But it should be noted that Betti's play provides no major premise, no minor premise and no conclusion. It is difficult to consider the absence of all three structural elements an enthymeme.

[21]Recent examples include Peter Weiss's West Berlin production of *The Investigation*, a play described as probing deeply into the German consciousness. The play dealt with the holocaust in a game-show setting, using the original courtroom exchanges from the 1965 Auschwitz trial in Frankfurt. Weiss used such examples as concentration camp doctors who dance tangos with their victims and titter when so-called medical experiments are described. The aim was apparently to awaken the Germans to the horror of their past, but one notes that no full argument was presented. Eve Merriam's *The Club* presented examples of male sexism using the unusual technique of having women portray men (some of whom at one point were women portraying men portraying women). Although fragments of argument appear, nothing resembling a complete discursive argument is found in the play.

[22]Thornton Wilder, "The Intent of the Artist," cited in Dukore, p. 891. Also, for an interesting discussion of discursive or expository writing in drama, see Thomas F. Van Laan, *The Idiom of Drama* (Ithaca: Cornell University Press, 1970), ch. 1.

[23]Ross, p. 58.

[24]Brockett and Findlay, pp. 502-508. Also, Oscar G. Brockett, *The Theatre: An Introduction*, third edition (New York: Holt, Rinehart and Winston, Inc., 1974), p. 43.

[25]See Susanne K. Langer, *Philosophy in a New Key: A Study in the Symbolism of Reason, Rite, and Art*, third edition (Cambridge: Harvard University Press, 1942), p. 97. For a treatment of "assimilation," see *Feeling and Form*, ch. 10.

[26]Gerald F. Else, *Aristotle's Poetics: the Argument*, p. 306.

[27]True, there are a few instances of theatre without dialogue. A recent example is Franz Xaver Kroetz' *Request Concert*, a one character piece in which a woman comes home from work, engages in various mundane activities, and finally kills herself. There are a few such oddities, but they seem to me to say little about the great mass of theatre that depends on language.

[28]Those groups that either work without playwrights or bring the playwright and the actors into the composing process still begin with the script. Whether it is written or oral, conceived by one person or many, there must be a plan for the performance. In the strict sense of the terms, *repetition* is impossible without a *script*.

[29]For what might be called an opposing movement, see Van Laan, p. 7.

[30]See Robert Findlay, "Grotowski's 'Cultural Explorations Bordering on Art, Especially Theatre,' " *Theatre Journal*, 32, 3 (October 1980), pp. 349-356.

[31]The following are among these authors: John Russell Brown, *Theatre Language: A Study of Arden, Osborne, Pinter, Wesker* (New York: Taplinger Publishing Company, 1972); Deirdre Burton, *Dialogue and Discourse: A Sociolinguistic Approach to Modern Drama Dialogue and Naturally Occurring Conversation* (Boston: Routledge & Kegan Paul, 1980); Jean Chothia, *Forging a Language: A Study of the Plays of Eugene O'Neill* (Cambridge: Cambridge University Press, 1979); Ruby Cohn, *Dialogue in American Drama* (Bloomington: Indiana University Press, 1971); Gareth Lloyd Evans, *The Language of Modern Drama* (Totawa, N.J.: Rowman and Littlefield, 1977); Andrew K. Kennedy, *Six Dramatists in Search of a Language* (London: Cambridge University Press, 1975); Elias Schwartz, *The Forms of Feeling: Toward a Mimetic Theory of Literature* (Port Washington, N.Y.: Kennikat Press, 1972); Bert O. States, *Irony and Drama: A Poetics* (Ithaca: Cornell University Press, 1971); Thomas F. Van Laan, *The Idiom of Drama* (Ithaca: Cornell University Press, 1970).

[32]Elias Schwartz, *The Forms of Feeling: Toward a Mimetic Theory of Literature* (Port Washington, N.Y.: Kennikat Press, 1972), especially ch. 1. Also, Jacques Maritain, *Redeeming the Time* (London: Geoffrey Bles: The Centenary Press, 1944), pp. 191-224.

[33]See Mel Gussow, "London to Broadway: How a Culture Shapes a Show," *The New York Times*, 3 February 1980, Section 2, p. 1.

[34]Serge Schmemann, " 'Gin Game': Happy Trip to Moscow," *The New York Times*, 23 June 1981, Section C, p. 7.

[35]For a discussion of these and other productions of *A Midsummer Night's Dream*, see *The Reader's Encyclopedia of Shakespeare*, edited by Oscar James Campbell (New York: Thomas Y. Crowell Company, 1966), pp. 546-548; Brockett and Findlay, pp. 219, 686-687; and the review by Patrick A. Farmer, *Theatre Journal*, 33, 3 (October 1981), pp. 405-406.

[36]In all disciplines, crafts, and arts, people revise and alter their materials, but it is only in theatre that the revisions and alterations are themselves part of the art form, along with the original (in the form of the text). Even the other performing arts lack this dimension, this reflexive function; for instance, Beethoven sonatas do not receive performances that are remotely comparable to the radically different productions given *A Midsummer Night's Dream*.

[37]Kenneth Burke, *Counter-Statement* (Berkeley: University of California Press, 1968), p. 124.

[38]Burke, *Counter-Statement*, p. 127.

[39]Burke, *Counter-Statement*, p. 46.

[40]Burke, *Counter-Statement*, pp. 142-143.

[41]Burke, *Counter-Statement*, p. 141.

[42]Burke, *Counter-Statement*, p. 141.

[43]Burke, *Counter-Statement*, pp. 141-142.

[44]Burke, *Counter-Statement*, p. 48.

[45]Burke, *Counter-Statement*, p. 46.

[46]I take these terms from Burk's *A Rhetoric of Motives* (Berkeley: University of California Press, 1969), pp. 20-23.

Chapter III

The Genres of Theatre

To claim that theatre is not a direct transaction between actors and audience, that theatre can present only those arguments ancillary to the examples on which it formally depends, that language is essential to the presentational form of the theatrical work, that such works often involve a creative tension between the text and the production, and that those works are unified by the direct and reverse functions of signs, images, and symbols is, of course, to say far too little. Questions arise regarding two major issues: first, the genres of works that shall be included in the world of the theatre, second, the differences between those genres. Both issues must be dealt with, and the two terms "theatre" and "drama" provide ready access to the first of these issues.

Theatre and Drama

Most dictionaries define drama something like this: "prose or verse compositions intended for performance on the stage, plays"; or, "prose or verse works written for or as if for performance by actors, plays." Such definitions make it clear that the works to be performed or intended for performance are synonymous with "plays." Further, the most common generic distinctions made today are those among poetry, prose fiction, and drama, the three being considered to make up the body of world literature. The history of these terms, so defined, goes back to Plato, who originated the theory of genre; he held that poets used narration when they spoke directly to their hearers without concealing themselves at all, that they used imitation when they put speeches in the mouths of characters, and that they used a mixed form when they combined the two or alternated between the one and the other.[1]

Paul Hernadi points out in *Beyond Genre*, a work indispensable to anyone concerned in any way with the matter of genre, that the move from Plato's *mimesis, diegesis*, and a combination of the two to the modern poetry, prose fiction, drama was anything but logical. Yet, by the beginning of this century it had become almost an article of faith that literary works had forever been classified as dramatic (*mimesis,* drama), lyric (*diegesis,* poetry), and epic (mixed style, prose fiction).[2] This tripartition is unsatisfactory for two major reasons, the first a broadly based critical objection, the second a problem that derives from the nature of performance.

While it was possible for Plato to identify the speaker or implied author of a work with its actual author, and hence to talk of poets hiding or revealing themselves, few critics today would claim that the voice, or *persona*, or speaker of a work is to be considered the actual author. There is far too much evidence, and evidence of a very direct sort, to the contrary. To cite but a single example, that whimsical, kindly, country philosopher seems to have had relatively little in common with Robert Frost, despite the frequency of his appearances in Frost's poems; a careful, authorized biography of the real Frost discloses a very different being.[3] And even when an author consistently uses one image or *persona*, there is little reason to believe that he or she is to be identified with that *persona*, as Hernadi, Eliot, Burke, and others have argued.[4] Of course, when an author creates many characters, he or she is, by definition, not to be identified with any of them. If Shakespeare *was* Hamlet, he must also have been Ophelia, Lear, Desdemona, Prospero, etc., which is to say he was none of them. Thus, Plato's identification of the author as the speaker or implied author of a work is no longer satisfactory.

But when the tie between author and *persona* is broken, a very important step is taken. As Wimsatt and Brooks put it, "Once we have dissociated the speaker of the lyric from the personality of the poet, even the tiniest lyric reveals itself as drama. A poem is not a 'statement about' something, but, as Aristotle said of tragedy, an *action*."[5] Both Cleanth Brooks and Kenneth Burke analyze "Ode on a Grecian Urn" as a dramatic structure.[6] Don Geiger holds that any piece of literature can be viewed as a dramatic form, the elements of which are identified by the questions Who? What? Where? When? How? Why?[7] For T. S. Eliot, "Poetry is essentially dramatic and the greatest poetry always moves toward drama; drama is essentially poetic and the greatest drama always moves toward poetry."[8] And it is not poetry alone that becomes dramatic in this fashion. When the novelist does not speak in her or his own person, when novels render what happens as action, when the narrator functions as a character in the work, or even when an omniscient narrator is speaking, we have novels that are dramas. Hernadi cites several theorists who describe particular novels as dramatic forms.[9] Various critics have used what would commonly be called nondramatic works as key illustrations in their discussions of drama: Eric Bentley often refers to novels and films;[10] Francis Fergusson uses the *Divine Comedy* as the key and continuing example of dramatic form.[11] It appears, then, that Plato's fusion of poet and *persona* must be rejected and that that rejection may result in a much broader concept of drama than is indicated by the term "play."

It was also possible for Plato to regard *mimesis, diegesis,* and the mixed form as kinds of performance, as modes in which the poet addressed the audience. But poetry, prose, and drama are not currently regarded as performance modes, and the second difficulty with these categories is one that develops out of the nature of performance as that process is understood and practiced today. If one takes the view that drama is that which is performable, that which can be turned into theatre, then there is a large amount of empirical evidence indicating that drama is by no means limited to so-called plays, but can often include essays, lyric poetry, parts of novels, letters, speeches, and what have you. Evidence for this claim is found in the long list of theatre events, usually one-person shows, made up of the writings, reminiscences, poetry, letters, etc., of famous people.[12] These events have varied in quality, of course, and one may wish to deny to certain of them a rightful place in the theatre (as one would deny that rightful place to certain plays), but many of them have been first rate works of theatre art: Julie Harris as Emily Dickinson, Hal Holbrook as Mark Twain, and Henry Fonda as Clarence Darrow, to name but three.

If drama is the raw material of theatre, such material apparently includes the essays, letters, poetry, etc., mentioned above, but the question arises with all these materials as to which is the "real" or complete dramatic form, the written work or the performed work. Hernadi points to the central issue when he says:

> I believe that a consistent logic of literature should either hold the view that dialogue *plus* staging constitute the finished product of dramatic art or else regard the entire written text (that is, the fictive dialogue *plus* the authorial statements of the 'side text') as an integrated, albeit not homogeneous, verbal structure.[13]

This statement is in striking contrast to the position held by Eric Bentley:

> Is a play complete without performance? The question has been answered with equal vehemence in both the affirmative and the negative. The choice goes by temperamental preference: "literary" persons believe in the unaided script; "theatrical" persons believe in performance. Both are right. A good play leads a double existence, and is a complete "personality" in both its lives.[14]

Hernadi's claim requires that one choose; Bentley's view relegates the choice to temperamental preference and allows one to say that theatre is both a literary and a performing art. But Bentley's logic quickly becomes tangled in its own traces, as when he argues that "even though the written script has its own completeness, there is no pleasure to top that of seeing a dramatic masterpiece masterfully performed. What is added means so much in such an immediate sensuous way..., above all by adding that final and conclusive concretion, the living actor."[15] If the playscript is in any sense complete in itself, how can performance add to it? Hernadi's view is, it seems to me, much the superior of the two; he does not deny that the playscript exists as a written work, for he says that "dramatic texts have been read even while their theatrical reproduction was neither feasible nor desired,"[16] and he describes as only "partially justified" the tendency of many theatre people "to regard the text of plays as a mere point of departure for the craft and imagination of performing artists."[17] Nevertheless, Hernadi allows the performed work much greater prominence and importance than does Bentley, despite the fact that he describes Bentley as "the most 'practical' drama critic surveyed"[18] in his book. Still, I want to go a bit further than Hernadi, as I have already indicated by describing the acting, directing, designing of a play as the completion of the written work.

Northrop Frye, perhaps the most systematic of generic critics, sets forth concepts of genre that permit one to place the performed work even more prominently than does Hernadi's comment, though I must emphasize that I am using Frye to my own ends here. Frye puts it in this manner: "The basis of generic distinctions in literature appears to be the radical of presentation. Words may be acted in front of a spectator; they may be spoken in front of a listener; they may be sung or chanted; or they may be written for a reader."[19] Here distinctions are made between the spoken word (*epos*), the acted word (drama), the sung or chanted word (lyric), and the written word (fiction). The first thing to note is that Frye takes the word "radical" very seriously; he emphasizes that "one may print a lyric or read a novel aloud, but such incidental changes are not enough in themselves to alter the genre."[20] This emphasis is particularly important to theatre people, for the mere fact that a script is a written document does not change its genre. Frye comments:

> A book, like a keyboard, is a mechanical device for bringing an entire artistic structure under the interpretive control of a single person. But just as it is possible to distinguish genuine piano music from the piano score of an opera or symphony, so we may distinguish genuine "book literature" from books containing the reduced textual scores of recited or acted pieces.[21]

In other words, scripts are written works and they may be read, but they are the scores, the reduced texts of the performed work. This is the point I was making in the section on language in the last chapter.

The second thing to note in Frye's distinctions among genres is that three of the four are modes of performance, that is, they are genres that were originally acted, spoken, or chanted. Thus, there is a very important sense in which one can say that there is the *performed* word (either acted, spoken, sung, or chanted) and the *written* word. And, indeed, Aristotle made precisely this distinction:

> The written style is the more finished: the spoken better admits of dramatic delivery—alike the kind of oratory that reflects of character and the kind that reflects emotion. Hence actors look out for plays written in the latter style, and poets for actors competent to act in such plays. Yet poets whose plays are meant to be read *are* read and circulated.[22]

Thus, Plato's three genres and the four-way distinction Frye makes can both be subsumed under a simple duality: performed word, written word. I have no interest in denying the distinctions that Frye makes, for they are of undoubted importance from various points of view, certainly from a historical vantage point. I *am* interested in proposing the simpler two-way distinction as one that is, in my judgment, important in regard to theatre, and I am interested because of what I take to be the reality, the pragmatics of theatre. For instance, one can surely draw the distinctions that Frye does, though it is by no means easy to do so;[23] any differences posited, while of historical worth, are likely to resolve themselves into matters of performance technique or style when regarded from a contemporary viewpoint. And when one considers the theatrical reality there for all to see, it appears that the issue of these generic distinctions and the issue of the limits of drama and theatre as performance arts can be approached quite simply.

For instance, there can be little disagreement that two or more actors, on stage, doing a scene from, say, *Othello* are engaged in something called acting a scene from a theatrical work. Let me now move away from that sort of obvious theatrical performance step by step in an attempt to see just how each move affects the nature of performance and the nature of theatre and drama.

If, instead of two or more actors, there is but one actor who performs a soliloquy from, say, *Macbeth*, is that actor no longer acting, and is it no longer theatre? The reasonable answer in such a case would seem to be that what one sees should still be called acting and theatre. There is the same sort of behavior going on; line-readings do not change simply because an actor is doing a monologue; stage movement is still involved; lighting, costumes, make-up, set design all continue to create a fictional scene in which the actor exists.

Now, instead of an actor doing a monologue or soliloquy, suppose that actor performs one of Robert Browning's dramatic monologues, "My

Last Duchess" or "Soliloquy of the Spanish Cloister." Is he or she no longer acting, and is this no longer theatre? So far as I can tell, there is no sound basis for saying so. The same techniques of performance can be used in these pieces as in the monlogues or the scenes from plays. And one can easily imagine the general sort of costume, set, and lighting that might be used in such performances. Indeed, such pieces are so obviously dramatic works that there may well be few objections to my claim so far. After all, the examples given are called *dramatic* monologues, even though they are also categorized as poems. Hence, as dramatic monologues they belong with such pieces as Chekhov's *On the Harmfulness of Tobacco,* a dramatic monologue that is not a poem.

The next steps, I suppose, would be to choose examples from narrative poetry and then descriptive poetry, but I shall skip these two and move straight to lyric poetry, for if lyric poetry can be demonstrated to be actable and theatrical, the others surely can. Imagine the hypothetical actor performing Elizabeth Barrett Browning's "How Do I Love Thee," not a piece usually thought of as theatrical. Of the examples given, the sex of the actor becomes significant here for the first time. We have been subjected (via a species of the intentional fallacy, I imagine) to what might be called an implied performer who is a woman. And certainly a woman could act the piece. One can easily imagine a romantic, tender, poeticized performance with the actor seated at an ornate writing-table or secretary in one corner of a bed-room; the room full of light colored gauzy drapes; the actor sitting still, perhaps looking at a picture of her beloved, and doing the reading with only one movement—she rises for the line "I love thee freely, as men strive for Right," taking a step or two away from the secretary then returns slowly to her seat for the last lines. But note that a very different performance is possible. A woman *or* a man could perform the work in a generally strong, robustly joyous fashion; the opening question read full voice, with a happy rise at the end, followed by a warm chuckle or even a delighted laugh; then the actor rises, walks around the room (a study, perhaps, overlooking a garden or stretch of lawn), emphasizes the ways he or she loves with broad, glad gestures; the line "I love thee freely, as men strive for Right," a happy and hearty declaration of passion; then a bit of a diminuendo toward the end, and the final "if God choose" line read with deliberate pauses as the actor comes downstage, smiling ("And...if God choose...I shall but love thee better...after death"); no mournful melancholy here, only a continuing joy. With the first performance, ideal casting would have a slender, graceful woman, with blonde or light brown hair and a quality that suggests, but just barely suggests, fragility; with the second performance, the woman or man should be large, strong looking, energetic, deep voiced, dark haired, with a quality of vibrancy and power.

Another lyric, Poe's "Annabel Lee." Here the clues about character, setting, and acting style are quite clear. The actor portrays a lover obsessed to the point of madness, as the work slowly makes clear. But the performance can begin sanely enough, the opening lines read simply, sadly, as if explaining a terrible puzzle to someone. With the second stanza, a bit more emphasis; the lines "With a love that the winged seraphs of heaven/Coveted her and me" should give the first hint of madness, the words uttered quite seriously, but with resentment apparent behind them. Then with the third stanza and the death and entombment of Annabel Lee, the tone changes, and the tragedy is related in mournful tones, with just a hint of the earlier resentment still present. But in the fourth stanza, the resentment bursts through with, "The Angels, not half so happy in heaven,/Went envying her and me./Yes! that was the reason (as all men know)/In this kingdom by the sea,/That the wind came out of the cloud by night,/Chilling and killing my Annabel Lee." The actor is claiming a kind of cosmic conspiracy here, and he should use a few of the keening intonations and odd aversions of the eye that will be central techniques at the end. With the fifth stanza, the madness becomes clearer; first there is the triumph over those older and wiser, then over both angels and demons, all of whom had joined in the conspiracy; the actor should have a glittering eye and a meaningless, crazed smile as he relates the triumph. And finally the complete madness, the character who lies down every night by the tomb of his love; the actor should here use to the full the keening tones, the strange, empty sideway looks, and the odd pauses that suggest madness. The setting is particularly interesting with this piece; a designer might create a set that gave the impression of a cell, a locked-in area, without any explicit details, but perhaps with shadows suggesting bars on the window. The costume, one that suggests an institution. The lighting, shadowy, with perhaps three more brightly lighted playing areas quite close together. Movement, the actor using pacing as a norm, pacing sometimes within one of the areas, sometimes from one area to another.

First: I am not arguing that these two works are *not* poems, simply that they *are* drama, that they can be performed, and that it is important for theatre people (and others) to so regard them. Second: I have fabricated these performance descriptions, but not out of whole cloth; I have seen each of these lyrics performed, though not in a fully orchestrated theatrical fashion. Third: In the performance of such works, is the actor still acting, and is the entire work properly called theatrical? My answer is an emphatic *yes.* I can see nothing so different between the performance of "Annabel Lee" and the performance of a scene from *Othello* as to cause the former to forfeit the name of acting, of drama, or of theatre. In both cases, there is a role for the actor to play, and in the playing the transformation from drama to theatre can occur. Fourth: Are these the only performances, the only stagings possible for "How Do I Love Thee" and "Annable Lee"? Certainly not. There is more than one way to perform or to stage *Othello* and *Macbeth*, and there is more than one performance approach that can be taken to any dramatic work. I do not even claim that these are the best or are among the best interpretations of these works; I am content to argue that they are legitimate interpretations. Fifth: If poems, stories, etc., are all performable, why are they not performed? Why don't we regularly spend evenings in the theatre viewing essays, lyrics, etc., instead of plays? One answer is that these various materials *are* performed, as I said earlier, though certainly not as often as plays. Another answer is based on the sheer pragmatics of theatre. No matter how illuminating or enriching a particular production of "When I Was One and Twenty" or "Stopping by Woods on a Snowy Evening" might be, the huge amount of time and energy needed to do sets, costume, and lighting would make that sort of production impractical. Weeks of work invested for a thirty second or one minute performance is not an attractive proposition for theatre people. Nor for audiences, for that matter. Of course, one could piece together a group of such short works, but then the question of continuity arises; such a production risks becoming a hodge-podge of unrelated items. And when the items *are* related, as by authorship, they *are* performed, at least on occasion.

Drama is that body of material that can be performed, that can be turned into theatre. Given works may never be performed for various practical reasons, but that should not lead one to claim that they are nondramatic. What makes drama is the implicit theatricality of a piece, the performability of the work. And if one asks what it is that make a work performable, the answer is the one I have already given: the presence of a role, a character, a *persona* for the actor to play. This is not an either/or matter, of course, for a *persona* may be strikingly clear or only dimly felt. The sharper and more forceful the *persona* the more performable the work.

One might go to the extreme of saying that all literature is drama, that all written works imply *personae* that can be enacted (the move Wimsatt and Brooks, Eliot, and Geiger have made explicitly or implicitly). Such a claim seems to follow from the notion that the separation of poet and *persona* means that drama is present. But though that extreme position has a certain satisfaction for a theatre person, I think that the facts of performance lead to the more modest view stated earlier: there is the performed word and there is the written word. Certain works are, I believe not suitable for performance. For one thing, the claims made earlier about the nature of argument in theatre constitute one sort of evidence leading to that conclusion. Typically, arguments do not allow themselves to be transformed into theatre, unless, that is, they are arguments that are secondary to other dramatic devices. This text, for instance, is not a dramatic form, nor are the Lincoln-Douglas debates (if presented on their own terms). Factors other than argument make a work ill-suited to performance. For instance, because of the sheer intricacy of the language, Joyce's *Finnegan's Wake* is a poor candidate for theatrical production. One simply needs to have time to go back and ponder on Joyce's language play. Finally, sheer length can make performance difficult, though one must be a bit tentative here, since there is no reason that a performance cannot be interrupted, perhaps by 45 minutes or so, as in the case of the Royal Shakespeare Company's production of *Nicholas Nickelby*,[24] perhaps by a day or more, as in the case of Alan Ayckbourne's three-part *The Norman Conquests*. But even so, it is hard to imagine a production of a complete version, not an abridged version, a complete version of *War and Peace.*

Thus, based on critical opinion (Eliot, Wimsatt and Brooks, Geiger, Burke, etc.) and on the empirical evidence offered by theatre practice, I propose that drama be considered that body of works that can be transformed into theatrical events. Works not capable of such transformation I would regard as literature in the strict sense. My purpose here is not to draw a hard and fast distinction between the two genres; like Frye, my aim is not so much sheer classification as it is clarification of similarities between kinds of works.[25] Nor am I in the least concerned to eliminate such concepts as "lyric," "narrative," "prose," "sonnet," etc. Any such attempt would be, at best, silly. I follow Hernadi in believing that multiple schemes of classification are needed.[26] For instance, I would argue that "Annabel Lee" is drama; and from my vantage point it is drama first and foremost, though others will wish to use different generic hierarchies. But it may be useful to superimpose on the notion of "Annabel Lee" as drama other concepts such as "poem," "lyric," etc.

A final point in this section: It seems very significant to me that there is empirical evidence for the claim that poems, letters, novels, etc., can be performed. As between *a priori* classifications that separate works into genres and the telling fact of theatrical pratice, I much prefer the latter. There is, I think, likely to be considerable discomfort for the critic who proclaims that a particular work is nondramatic literature and then sees that work well and effectively performed in the theatre. Confronted with various types of material that are performed, it would seem unwise to ignore the fact of such performances.

Tragedy and Comedy
Any attempt to deal with the world of theatre must confront the terms

"tragedy" and "comedy." They are at least as old as dramatic theory and criticism, if not as theatre itself. These are the genres into which the works of theatrical art are most frequently separated. Let me begin by giving some definitions of these terms; the most famous and most frequently cited is, of course:

> Tragedy, then, is an imitation of an action that is serious, complete, and of a certain magnitude; in language embellished with each kind of artistic ornament, the several kinds being found in separate parts of the play; in the form of action, not of narrative; through pity and fear effecting the proper purgation of these emotions.[27]

Aristotle gives no similar, concise definition of comedy, but one can piece together a definition of sorts: Comedy is an imitation of an action that is laugh-provoking rather than serious; it imitates characters of a type worse than in life[28] (as opposed to those better than in life imitated by tragedy); its characters are ludicrous but not painfully ugly;[29] and its plot may be double (as opposed to the unity of action of tragedy), with characters who may meet various fates and even with enemies becoming friends.[30]

Dante expresses this view:

> [Comedy] differs from tragedy in its matter in this respect, that tragedy in the beginning is good to look upon and quiet, in its end or exit is fetid and horrid;... Comedy, however, at the beginning deals with the harsh aspect of some affair, but its matter terminates prosperously,....[31]

Thomas Heywood argues in a similar vein:

> Tragedies and comedies...differ thus: in comedies *turbulenta prima, tranquilla ultimata;* in tragedies *tranquilla prima, turbulenta ultima;* comedies begin in trouble and end in peace; tragedies begin in calms and end in tempest.[32]

Giovambattista Giraldi Cinthio writes this:

> [Comedy and tragedy] have a common purpose in that both attempt to inculcate good morals. However,...their methods are different. Comedy exists without terror and without commiseration (because there are no interruptions of deaths or other terrible accidents; on the contrary, comedy seeks to bring about its conclusion through pleasure and with some funny jokes). And whether it has a happy ending or an unhappy one, tragedy—through the representation of extreme suffering and terrifying events—purges the spectators of vices and inculcates good morals....[33]

Henri Bergson holds that it is the characters that constitute the important distinction between tragedy and comedy; "the hero of a tragedy represents an individuality unique of its kind," while writers of comedy create a central character and then "cause other characters, displaying the same general traits, to revolve as satellites around him"; thus, the "essential difference between tragedy and comedy" is that the former is "concerned with individuals and the latter with classes."[34]

August Wilhelm von Schlegel argues that "the *tragic* and *comic* bear the same relation to one another as *earnest* and *sport*,"[35] the former being the frame of mind in which one examines the limitless possibilities that may come to pass and realizes one's helplessness in regard to them, the latter the state of mind in which one concentrates on present happiness and ignores whatever might mar that pleasant concentration.

Kierkegaard puts it provocatively: "The tragic and the comic are the same, insofar as both are based on contradiction; but *the tragic is the suffering contradiction, the comical, the painless contradiction.*"[36]

And Eugène Ionesco says this: "It seems to me that comic and tragic are one, and that the tragedy of man is pure derision," and he goes on to state that he has tried to bring the two together but that "these two elements do not coalesce, they coexist: one constantly repels the other, they show each other up, criticize and deny one another and, thanks to their opposition, thus succeed dynamically in maintaining a balance and creating tension."[37]

There are hundreds of other definitions and descriptions (Hernadi cites and comments on many of the most interesting ones[38]). I give these examples to show, first, that the world of the theatre has from a very early period been divided into tragedies and comedies, second, that many of these definitions include or emphasize theme or content (e.g., Aristotle's superior or inferior characters, Dante's horrible or prosperous endings, Cinthio's terrifying events), and third, that there has long been a simultaneous synthesis and division between tragedy and comedy (most clearly seen in Ionesco's statements, but also apparent in Aristotle's focus on the characters imitated in both, in Cinthio's purpose common to both, and in Kierkegaard's notion that both are based on contradiction). This third point has led many theorists to talk of a mixed form and to stress the fact that tragedy and comedy are not simple, independent genres. Indeed, anyone who subscribed to the idea of a clear separation between tragedy and comedy on the basis of content or theme would at once be forced to account for such works as *The Chalk Garden, Equus, Betrayal, Da, Gemini, The Gin Game, Our Town, Company, Sweeney Todd,* to mention but a few modern examples. None of these is easily categorized as tragedy or comedy on the basis of content. And such balky instances confront one all the way back to Sophocles' *Philoctetes* and Euripides' *Alcestis* and *Iphigenia in Tauris*.

But theme or content is not the only ground for the generic

classification of theatrical works; *form* provides an alternative basis for categorization, and there are important elements of form in most of the definitions cited above (e.g., the imitation of an action in Aristotle, the change from quiet to turmoil [or vice versa] in both Dante and Heywood, the presence of contradicton in Kierkegaard and the simultaneous attracting and repelling of the two genres in Ionesco). However, the theorist who has done what is, to my mind, the most significant work with the formal elements of tragedy and comedy is Susanne Langer. To summarize very briefly the argument that Langer spells out carefully and at considerable length, the world of art is a world of created forms, "forms symbolic of human feeling";[39] each of these forms "negotiates insight, not reference; it does not rest upon convention, but motivates and dictates conventions. It is deeper than any semantic of accepted signs and their referents, more essential than any schema that may be heuristically read";[40] and each of these forms is entirely real, though it is a reality of a special sort that Langer calls semblance or virtual reality, a created object given entirely to the senses or the imagination.[41] *Poesis* is the group of arts that creates the kind of semblance or virtual reality Langer refers to variously as "virtual life," "virtual experience," or "the illusion of life."[42] The poetic arts are literature, drama, and film; all create virtual life or experience, literature in the mode of memory or of a virtual past, film in the mode of dream or of a virtual present, and drama in the mode of destiny or of a virtual future.[43] Literature "is 'like' memory in that it is projected to compose a finished experiential form, a 'past' "; "drama is 'like' action in being causal, creating a total imminent experience, a personal 'future' or Destiny"; "cinema is 'like' dream in the mode of its presentation: it creates a virtual present, an order of direct apparition."[44]

Langer separates drama from literature very sharply: "Drama is not, in the strict sense, 'literature' "; "drama is not merely a distinct literary form; it is a special poetic mode, as different from genuine literature as sculpture from pictorial art, or either of these from architecture."[45] The fundamental difference between literature and drama is that the basic abstraction of the former is the *event*, while the abstraction basic to the latter is the *act*.[46]

Having set off drama from literature, Langer begins the process of distinguishing between tragedy and comedy. Her first key statement is this:

> Drama abstracts from reality the fundamental forms of consciousness: the first reflection of natural activity in sensation, awareness, and expectation, which belongs to all higher creatures and might be called, therefore, the pure sense of life; and beyond that, the reflection of an activity which is at once more elaborate and more integrated, having a beginning, efflorescence, and end—the

personal sense of life, or self-realization. The latter probably belongs only to human beings, and to them in varying measure.[47]

Here is the form of drama, the form realized only in the theatre: the sensation, awareness, and expectation, the pure sense of life that one finds in comedy; the personal or individual sense of life found in tragedy.

Langer continues to differentiate between the two forms in this manner: comedy reflects the pure sense of life, the incomparably complex process of living in a complicated and puzzling world in which the protagonist knows that "even the dead may still play into his life"; given this vast puzzle, "mental adroitness is [the protagonist's] chief asset for exploiting it"; what is needed, therefore, is "a brainy opportunism in face of an essentially dreadful universe."[48] In sum:

> This human life-feeling is the essence of comedy. It is at once religious and ribald, knowing and defiant, social and freakishly individual. The illusion of life which the comic poet creates is the oncoming future fraught with dangers and opportunities, that is, with physical or social events occurring by chance and building up the coincidences with which individuals cope according to their lights. This ineluctable future—inelectuable because its countless factors are beyond human knowledge and control—is Fortune. Destiny in the guise of Fortune is the fabric of comedy; it is developed by comic action, which is the upset and recovery of the protagonist's equilibrium, his contest with the world and his triumph by wit, luck, personal power, or even humorous, or ironical, or philosophical acceptance of mischance. Whatever the theme—serious and lyrical as in *The Tempest*, coarse slapstick as in the *Schwänke* of Hans Sachs, or clever and polite social satire—the immediate sense of life is the underlying feeling of comedy, and dictates its rhythmically structured unity, that is to say its organic form.[49]

It should be noted that the form of comedy is shown in the nature and behavior of its characters. Comedy is not a matter of tone or atmosphere, those undeniably important but relatively intangible elements about which critics can so easily disagree. Comedy is a matter of structure, of form. Its personages persevere in the face of misfortune, recover from upsets, and do battle with the world, sometimes using the witty tangle of their minds, sometimes the sheer dogged ability to survive. And survive they must; comic protagonists need not prevail, but they must survive.

Tragedy, by contrast, reveals life, "not merely as a process, but as a career. This career of the individual is variously conceived as a 'calling,' the attainment of an ideal, the soul's pilgrimage, 'life's ideal,' or self-realization."[50] In other words:

> Tragedy dramatizes human life as potentiality and fulfillment. Its virtual future, or Destiny, is therefore quite different from that created in comedy. Comic Destiny is Fortune—what the world will bring, and the man will take or

miss, encounter or escape; tragic Destiny is what the man brings, and the world will demand of him. That is his Fate.[51]

Both tragedy and comedy deal with destiny, but destiny viewed "as a future shaped essentially in advance and only incidentally by chance happenings, is Fate; and Fate is the 'virtual future' created in tragedy."[52] And finally:

> The 'tragic rhythm of action,' as Professor Fergusson calls it, is the rhythm of a man's life at its highest powers in the limits of his unique, death-bound career. Tragedy is the image of Fate, as comedy is of Fortune. Their basic structures are different; comedy is essentially contingent, episodic, and ethnic; it expresses the continuous balance of sheer vitality that belongs to society and is exemplified briefly in each individual; tragedy is a fulfillment, and its form therefore is closed, final, and passional.[53]

Several things should be noted about these remarks. For one, tragedy is like comedy in that its form is apparent in the nature and behavior of its leading characters. The tragic protagonist is shown as he or she "grows, flourishes and declines,"[54] engaging in "a characteristically human action...exemplified in mental and emotional growth, maturation, and the final relinquishment of power";[55] in brief, "tragic action is the realization of all [the protagonist's] possibilities, which he unfolds and exhausts in the course of the drama."[56] Tragic form, then, is not hidden but is readily accessible to critical examination.

Also, to restate the obvious, Langer bases her genres on form and not on content. She makes this abundantly clear when she says, " 'The tragic theme' and 'the comic theme'—guilt and expiation, vanity and exposure— are not the essence of drama, not even the determinants of its major forms, tragedy and comedy; they are means of dramatic construction, and as such they are, of course, not indispensable, however widespread their use."[57] It is not theme but form that is the mark of tragedy or comedy, a basic structure that is essentially contingent, episodic, and ethnic or is closed, final, and passional.

Next, like most other theorists, Langer does not regard the forms of tragedy and comedy as independent and unrelated; she sees the difference between them as radical, but adds that it is "a difference which is, however, not one of opposites—the two forms are perfectly capable of various combinations, incorporating elements of one in the other. The matrix of the work is always either tragic or comic; but within its frame the two often interplay."[58]

Finally, though the over-all configuration of the comments Langer makes on tragedy and comedy is original, several of the specific points she raises have been made by others. The notion of tragedy reflecting the pattern of one life conceived as a career is quite similar to Aristotelian doctrine: commenting on the *Poetics*, Else writes, "Aristotle is almost the only ancient critic (besides Plato) to make tragedy an imitation of 'life' also. Now $\beta\acute{\iota}o\varsigma$, unlike $\zeta\omega\acute{\eta}$, carries from the beginning the connotation of a *career*; the life of man seen as a single entity, from one vantage-point, or at least as a single span."[59] In the separation of drama from literature, Langer's position is essentially that of Elder Olson,[60] J.L. Styan,[61] Elmer Rice,[62] Brander Matthews,[63] Francis Fergusson,[64] and others; some of these writers preceded Langer's formulation of the concept, others followed it. And the idea of tragedy and comedy existing in combination was made explicit at least as early as Plautus, who, perhaps facetiously, labeled his own *Amphitryon* a *tragicomoedia* because of its mixture of kings, gods, and humble folk. Last of all, Langer's crucial point on comedy as either humorous or serious has been stated by others, e.g., Scaliger,[65] Castelvetro,[66] Jonson,[67] Diderot,[68] Schlegel,[69] etc. But Langer applies this concept tellingly. She mentions as examples of comedy the serious and lyrical theme of *The Tempest* and the coarse slapstick of Hans Sachs' *Schwänke*, and, in more general terms, she says, "There is heroic drama, romantic drama, political drama, all in the comic pattern, yet entirely serious; the 'history' is usually exalted comedy."[70] Serious comedy is, perhaps, most frequently found in Asia,[71] but it is an important form in the European tradition, where "the Spanish *Comedia* was perhaps its only popular and extended development."[72] As for specific plays and playwrights, "Corneille and Racine considered their dramas tragedies, yet the rhythm of tragedy—the growth and full realization of a personality—is not in them; the Fate their personages meet is really misfortune, and they meet it heroically."[73] Also, "romantic drama such as Schiller's *Wilhelm Tell* illustrates the same principle. It is another species of serious heroic comedy. Tell appears as an exemplary personage in the beginning of the play...and the Gessler episode merely gives him opportunity to show his indomitable skill and daring."[74] Langer says that such instances of serious comedy are "its rarer examples,"[75] but I would emphasize that they are frequent enough and important enough to make this a significant concept in a theory of comedy.

Langer's ideas about tragedy and comedy are valuable because they work, because they illuminate theatrical works in very important ways. She has already pointed to works by Shakespeare, Corneille, Racine and others as examples of serious comedy, and that very generic placement of the plays makes possible a degree of understanding often missing in the treatment of these works by other theorists. And further applications come to mind immediately. For example, Joseph Wood Krutch would deny that *Death of a Salesman* is a tragedy because of the lack of the quality of nobility in that play's characters and their actions,[76] but if one employs

Langer's concepts, one sees that the play is clearly tragic, not because of Willy Loman's death, but because he spent himself in the pursuit of success as a salesman and as a husband and father. Beckett's *Waiting for Godot* is often called a tragicomedy, but the structure of the play is clearly comic, the upset and recovery of the protagonists and the sense of continuing life that they reflect. Chekhov's four great plays are among those most widely regarded as tragicomedies, but Langer's concepts show that there are very important differences among them. *The Three Sisters* is formally a comedy in that none of the major characters changes significantly during the play; they all recover from the blows of fortune and go on, and this is especially true of the sisters. There is a minor tragic dimension in that the Prozorov home as a kind of community where the officers and others gather regularly has declined and come to an end. Chance determines most of the events, even the Baron's death. Much of the play is wildly humorous, with characters constantly talking past each other, but there is also a consistent strain of seriousness. *The Cherry Orchard* is also a comedy in formal terms, for all the characters exhibit the continuity and the ability to spring back from fortune's blows that are the marks of the comic rhythm. But there is an important formal element that is tragic; the estate has been sold, and the family no longer has its place; this is a somewhat stronger version of the end of the Prozorov home as a community in *The Three Sisters.* There is much use of humor in *The Cherry Orchard,* but there is also the sadness of the sale of the estate. And though chance is an important factor here (Ranevsky, for example, always depends on the kindness of fortune), there is also a sense in which things are foreordained, for the sale of the estate could have been prevented but was not because of the character of Ranevsky, Gayev, and the others, i.e., their mode of existence made inevitable the loss of the state. *Uncle Vanya* is formally a comedy, though one that is serious (even didactic) in considerable part. The characters Vanya and Sonia reflect the continuing vitality of the comic rhythm. At the same time, those two characters exist in a tragic dimension, for their awareness of Serebryakov's shallowness and his willingness to sell the estate means the loss of innocence and the end of their earlier life. Other tragic patterns include Sonia's unrequited love for Astrov which brings her to a small death, and even the loss of some of Serebryakov's (and Yelena's) power over the others. Chance is a factor here, too, but neither the discovery of Serebryakov's foolishness nor his quite ugly readiness to dispossess the others is a matter of chance at all. Finally, *The Seagull* is formally a tragedy. Konstantin is a tragic character through and through; his fight to be a writer and his love for Nina show the classic pattern of birth, growth and finally death. Nina operates in a tragic frame in that her affair with Trigorin dies, and her career seems to be sliding slowly toward its own decline. Masha and Medvenko display the tragic rhythm insofar as their marriage is a failure. And Sorin, of course, is slowly dying. Indeed, Arkadina and Trigorin are the only nontragic characters. Chance plays no major role here, and there is a very limited use of humor in comparison with the other three plays.

One more example, and a very different one: A study of the Stephen Sondheim musical comedy, *Sweeny Todd: The Demon Barber of Fleet Street*, reveals strikingly the strengths of Langer's concepts. *Sweeney Todd* is a work with many strengths, but several major weaknesses. First, the music is not assimilated into the comic structure in a way that permits the work to function as a musical comedy, and critics, perhaps, had this in mind when they talked of the work as more nearly opera than musical comedy. The American form we call musical comedy is structurally comedy, comedy that uses music for dramatic purposes.[77] But in the case of *Sweeney Todd*, important parts of the work remain unassimilated, remain musical forms, e.g., the long duet between the young lovers in the first act. Second, *Sweeney Todd* is structurally a tragedy, with only secondary elements of comedy (though Angela Lansbury's broad comedy performance techniques disguised much of this truth). The rhythm of development is tragic through and through. Sweeney Todd spends his powers in an attempt at revenge, only to find at the end that he has killed his lost love. Even Mrs. Lovett moves in a tragic rhythm, for she strives to attract Sweeney, but ends in her own oven. In other words, *Sweeney Todd* is structurally a musical tragedy (though music is not assimilated to the tragic form either). And as soon as one looks at the show in that light, one sees its weaknesses quite clearly: lack of congruence between the form of the work and performance style; far too much emphasis on the peripheral characters Johanna and Anthony; and a use of physical production elements, e.g., the enormous set, that had nothing at all to do with what was going on in the play most of the time. Nor is the concept of serious comedy useful here; the episodic, upset and recovery, on-going rhythm of life is not the structure of this work.

Langer's critical concepts work when applied to specific tragedies and comedies, and they work because they allow one to focus on the characters of a play and to use the characters and their actions in placing the work generically. The simple fact of theatre is that if a playwright skillfully combines two tragic characters whose development is marked by a beginning, efflorescence, and end, and one comic character whose behavior expresses the continuous balance of sheer vitality, her or his play is a tragedy that includes a major comic dimension (the combination of characters must, of course, be *skillfully* done), and Langer's approach to genre permits one to recognize this simple fact. Further, Langer's concepts work with the over-all genre of drama discussed earlier in the chapter. That is, even such forms as "Annabel Lee" and "How Do I Love Thee" are part of the genre called drama because they offer parts for the actor to play, and they are, therefore, appropriately classed as tragedies or comedies, tragedy in the case of "Annabel Lee," serious but joyful comedy in the case of "How Do I Love Thee." The one-person shows I have mentioned succeeded when they did because an editor or director arranged small works into an over-all tragic or comic form (nearly always comedy or tragedy with major elements of comedy); and they failed when they did because those works were not arranged in any clear over-all structure, but presented odds and ends of a personality rather than a fully drawn character.

Drama is that which can be transformed into theatre. The genres of tragedy and comedy include materials other than plays. Susanne Langer's treatment of these two forms as contingent, episodic, and ethnic, in the case of comedy, and closed, final, and passional, in the case of tragedy, offers valuable working concepts to the dramatic theorist or critic. Langer's works are, of course, widely read, but they have received too little attention by theatre people; there is but a handful of dissertations, journal articles, and books that deal at any length with Langer's ideas.

Notes

[1]Plato *Republic* 3. 392c-394c.

[2]Paul Hernadi, *Beyond Genre: New Directions in Literary Classification* (Ithaca: Cornell University Press, 1972), p. 55.

[3]See Lawrance Roger Thompson, *Robert Frost:* Vol. 1, *The Early Years*, 1874-1915; Vol. 2, *The Years of Triumph*, 1915-1938; Vol. 3, *The Later Years*, 1938-1963.

[4]See Hernadi, pp. 82-83.

[5]William K. Wimsatt, Jr. and Cleanth Brooks, *Literary Criticism: A Short History* (New York: Random House, 1957), pp. 675-676.

[6]Cleanth Brooks, *The Well Wrought Urn: Studies in the Structure of Poetry* (New York: Harcourt, Brace and Company, 1947), pp. 151-166; Kenneth Burke, *A Grammar of Motives* (Berkeley: University of California Press, 1969), pp. 447-463.

[7]Don Geiger, *The Sound, Sense, and Performance of Literature* (Chicago: Scott, Foresman and Company, 1963) ch. 6.

[8]Cited in Wimsatt and Brooks, p. 694. Eliot's belief is, perhaps, a bit idiosyncratic.

[9]Hernadi, pp. 41, 63-65.

[10]References are scattered through Bentley's *The Life of the Drama.*

[11]Francis Fergusson, *The Idea of A Theatre* (Garden City, N.Y.: Doubleday Anchor Books, by arrangement with Princeton University Press, 1953).

[12]Theatrical works have been created out of the speeches, letters, poetry, books, and what have you of Casey Stengel, St. Mark and various Biblical characters, Dickens, H. L. Mencken, Eudora Welty, Mark Twain, Emily Dickinson, President Truman, Will Rogers, Walt Whitman, Clarence Darrow, and many others. See *The New York Times* of 22 April 1981, p. C19; 7 May 1981, p. C19; 14 May 1981, p. C21; 15 January 1981, p. C20; 10 August 1980, p. 50; 3 October 1980, p. C16; 23 October 1980, p. C20; 23 June 1980, p. C12; 3 June 1980, p. C18; 9 March 1980, p. D4.

[13]Hernadi, pp. 50-51.

[14]Bentley, p. 148.

[15]Bentley, p. 149.

[16]Hernadi, p. 76.

[17]Hernadi, p. 76.

[18]Hernadi, p. 108.

[19]Northrop Frye, *Anatomy of Criticsm* (New York: Atheneum, 1967), pp. 246-247.

[20]Frye, p. 247. There is some confusion on this point, however, for Frye also says, "The novels of Dickens are, as books, fiction; as serial publications in a magazine designed for family reading, they are still fundamentally fiction, though closer to *epos*. But when Dickens began to give readings from his own works, the genre changed wholly to *epos;* the emphasis was thrown on immediacy of effect before a visible audience"(249). Here it seems that reading a novel aloud *was* enough to alter the genre.

[21]Frye, p. 248.

[22]Aristotle *Rhetoric* 3. 12. 1413b9-12.

[23]So far as contemporary modes of performance are concerned, the area of Oral Interpretation (sometimes located in theatre departments, more frequently in departments of speech communication) has for a good many years attempted to differentiate between oral recitation or oral interpretation and acting. That attempt has not been very successful, though I should mention that I have been one of those who has argued against such a differentiation.

[24]This is a very interesting case of a production with many strengths, but one that failed to provide the examples central to theatre and that, therefore, became nondramatic at times. See Robert Brustein, "In the Constructive Element, Immerse," *The New Republic*, October 28, 1981, pp. 25-26; Walter Kerr, "Surrendering To 'Nicholas Nickleby,' " *The New York Times*, 18 October 1981, Section D, p. 3; Frank Rich, "Why 'Nickleby' Is Potent but Flawed," *The New York Times*, 11 October 1981, Section D, p. 1; Frank Rich, "Stage: 'Nicholas Nickleby' Arrives As a Two-Part, 8½-Hour Drama," Section C, p. 13.

[25]Frye, p. 247.

[26]Hernadi, p. 153.

[27]Aristotle *Poetics* 6. 1449b24-28.

[28]*Poetics* 3. 1448a16-18.

[29]*Poetics* 5. 1449a31-36.

[30]*Poetics* 13. 1453a37-39.

[31]Dante, "Letter to Can Grande Della Scala," cited in *Literary Criticism: Plato to Dryden*, edited by Allan H. Gilbert (Detroit: Wayne State University Press, 1962), pp. 203-204.

[32]Thomas Heywood, *An Apology for Actors*, Book III, cited in Gilbert, p. 555.

[33]Giovambattista Giraldi Cinthio, *Discourse on Comedies and Tragedies*, cited in Bernard F. Dukore, *Dramatic Theory and Criticsm: Greeks to Grotowski* (New York: Holt, Rinehart and Winston, Inc., 1974), p. 121.

[34]Henri Bergson, *Laughter: an Essay on the Meaning of the Comic*, cited in *Literary Criticsm: Pope to Croce*, edited by Gary Wilson Allen and Harry Hayden Clark (Detroit: Wayne State University Press, 1962), p. 620.

[35]August Wilhelm von Schlegel, *Lectures on Dramatic Art and Literature*, cited in Dukore, p. 499.

[36]Søren Kierkegaard, *Concluding Unscientific Postscript*, cited in Dukore, p. 556.

[37]Eugene Ionesco, *Notes and Counter-Notes*, cited in Dukore, p. 771.

[38]Hernadi, pp. 93-113.

[39]Susanne K. Langer, *Feeling and Form* (New York: Charles Scribner's Sons, 1953), p. 40.

[40]*Feeling and Form*, p. 22.

[41]*Feeling and Form*, ch. 4.

[42]*Feeling and Form*, chs. 15-17 and Appendix.

[44]*Feeling and Form*, p. 412. For an interesting objection to this view of the three genres, see Bert O. States, *Irony and Drama* (Ithaca: Cornell University Press, 1971), pp. 19-22.

[45]*Feeling and Form*, p. 306.

[46]*Feeling and Form*, pp. 306-307.

[47]*Feeling and Form*, p. 327.

[48]*Feeling and Form*, pp. 330-331.

[49]*Feeling and Form*, p. 331.

[50]*Feeling and Form*, p. 333.

[51]*Feeling and Form*, p.352.

[52]*Feeling and Form*, p. 333.

[53]*Feeling and Form*, pp. 333-334.

[54]*Feeling and Form*, p. 356.

[55]*Feeling and Form*, p. 356.

[56]*Feeling and Form*, p. 352.

[57]*Feeling and Form*, p. 326-327.

[58]*Feeling and Form*, p. 334.

[59]Else, p. 257.

[60]Elder Olson, *Tragedy and the Theory of Drama* (Detroit: Wayne State University Press, 1966), pp. 8-9, 12-13.

[61]J. L. Styan, *Drama, Stage and Audience* (London: Cambridge University Press, 1975), p. vii.

[62]Rice, pp. 14-15.

[63]Matthews, pp. 1-4.

[64]Fergusson, pp. 21-22.

[65]Julius Caesar Scaliger, *Poetics*, excerpted in Barrett H. Clark, *European Theories of the Drama*, edited by Henry Popkin (New York: Crown Publishers, Inc., 1965), pp. 46-47.

[66]Lodovico Castelvetro, *Poetics*, excerpted in Clark, p. 49.

[67]Ben Jonson, *Timber: Or Discoveries Made upon Men and Matter*, excerpted in Clark, p. 77.

[68]Denis Diderot, *On Dramatic Poetry*, excerpted in Clark, p. 239.

[69]Schlegel, cited in Clark, p. 288.

[70]*Feeling and Form*, p. 334.

[71]*Feeling and Form*, p. 335. See also p. 337, n. 9.

[72]*Feeling and Form*, p. 336.

[73]*Feeling and Form*, p. 336. Hernadi says this view of Corneille and Racine is "overingenious" (107).

[74]*Feeling and Form*, p.338.

[76]See Joseph Wood Krutch, *The Tragic Fallacy*, in Dukore, pp. 868-880.

[77]For a study of Langer's concepts as applied to musical comedy and specifically to *Sweeney Todd*, see James B. Graves, "A Theory of Musical Comedy Based on the Concepts of Susanne K. Langer," Diss. University of Kansas 1981, especially pp. 231-244.

Part II
Dramatic Criticism

Chapter IV

Dramatic Criticism: Object and Method

At the start of this chapter, I want to repeat what I said in the Introduction: strictly speaking, theory and criticism are not separate processes, for good criticism brings with it new theoretical formulations from time to time, and sound theory involves critical insights into particular works. Nevertheless, I have followed common practice and divided this essay into two parts, and, with the above caveat, I shall follow the distinction between theory as the fomulation of general concepts and criticism as the application of those concepts to specific artworks.

In preceding chapters, I have argued 1) that the performed work has its own objective reality and is not dependent on any particular audience or audience response, but that 2) performances are designed for and directed to virtual audiences; 3) that the most obvious of the formal elements that make up theatre are the characters, the virtual speakers; 4) that dramatic works, especially when completed in the theatre, are presentational and not discursive forms, and 5) these presentational forms rely on the example as their chief formal element, using argument only in secondary capacities; 6) that because theatre cannot argue in the full sense, it is sharply limited in its subject matter and in the ways it can treat that subject matter; 7) that language is essential to theatre, is the element that results when one goes through the process of abstracting from the performed work, and is the only element of theatre that has artistic status (albeit incomplete) in its own right; 8) that the verbal and nonverbal, discursive and presentational elements of theatre are unified into wholes, into artworks that have their own identity and are not simply mixtures of other arts; 9) that the formal elements of theatre are implied in the text, but come into full being only in production, and, hence, the form of production can work with or against the form of the text; 10) that drama is that which is performable, that which can be turned into theatre, and 11) that drama includes many works other than plays; 12) that tragedy and comedy are to be defined in terms of form, not in terms of theme or content, and 13) that (following Langer) comedy reflects the sense of life via the protagonist's recoveries from upsets that fortune deals out, 14) tragedy the sense of a career or personal mission via the protagonist's expenditure of her or himself in meeting the demands of fate.

These items are, as I said, general constructs. They are, in the main, descriptive rather than prescriptive (though there are elements of prescription in several of them, e.g., nos. 12, 13, 14). Because of their generality and their descriptive nature, they provide an over-all frame of reference, but *they do not equip one to make specific comments about specific productions of dramatic works.* All these concepts do is to assure one that the work being criticized *is* a dramatic form capable of being turned into a theatrical event. That is as it should be, of course, for a theoretical base that required particular pronouncements about individual works-in-performance would merit the disdain that I argued in the Introduction is not deserved by dramatic theory and criticism. Thus, the critic must move far beyond the fourteen general formulations I have listed, for it will hardly qualify as criticism if he or she merely claims that this or that or the other performed work depends on the example, or displays a comic structure, or uses language in an important way. What the critic must do is to turn these general concepts into specifics in her or his application of them. Individual works must be singled out and their strengths or weaknesses made clear, and to accomplish that, the critic must engage in three interrelated endeavors which together make up the critical process.[1] The critic must *describe, interpret,* and *evaluate,* and in all three processes must use an appropriate *vocabulary.* First, some comments about that vocabulary.

The Critical Vocabulary

With any sort of criticism, it is essential to use a vocabulary that is suited to the works being criticized. Key terms must point one in the right critical direction and keep one headed in that direction. I talked of Burke's "terministic screens" in the Introduction, and it is that concept I want to return to here. Burke provides a vocabulary that is, in my judgment, essentially theatrical and is, therefore, particularly suited to dramatic criticism. Burke's cluster of key terms is found in what he calls the pentad: Act, Scene, Agent, Agency, Purpose.[2] This is an extremely flexible critical tool: Act is a term that can be used to deal with the actor's behavior, with the actions of a character, with the playwright's creation of the script, with the plot line of the play, etc.; Scene can refer to the physical sets, lights, etc., to the fictive world of the play, or to the actual theatre in which performances are given, and even to the period in which a play is performed or written; Agent can mean actor, or character, or playwright; Agency is a term that can be used to refer to language when employed instrumentally, or to the physical and nonphysical items used by characters as they engage in action; and Purpose can mean the reason for the character's action, the actor's motivation, or the goal toward which the development of the play proceeds.[3] Burke emphasizes the presence of these dramatic elements in all sorts of works (further support for the broad view of drama proposed in the last chapter). Regarding Scene, he says this:

> The nature of the scene may be conveyed primarily by suggestions built into the lines of the verbal action itself, as with the imagery in the dialogue of Elizabethan drama and with the descriptive passages of novels; or it may be conveyed by non-linguistic properties, as with the materials of naturalistic stage-sets.[4]

Beyond their ubiquity, Burke stresses the ties or "ratios" between these key terms, and it is in regard to the theatre that Burke makes this point most strongly:

> Thus, when the curtain rises to disclose a given stage-set, this stage-set contains, simultaneously, implicitly, all that the narrative is to draw out as a sequence, explicitly. Or, if you will, the stage-set contains the action *ambiguously* (as regards the norms of action)—and in the course of the play's development this ambiguity is converted into a corresponding *articulacy*. The proportion would be: scene is to act as implicit is to explicit. One could not deduce the details of the action from the details of the setting, but one could deduce the quality of the action from the quality of the setting.[5]

This is the kind of integrated, organic view that is likely to please many theatre people, and I will have more to say on the matter of ratios between the terms in just a bit.

It is important to understand that I am not proposing a *second* theoretical structure to go with the one already set down. Rather, Burke's vocabulary grows out of that list of fourteen items because it was implicit in them from the very start. To talk in any way of performance, of enactment, of the production as a form that modifies the script is to deal with Act; to discuss characters, or actors, or virtual speakers is to work with Agent; to describe the stage, or the physical theatre, or the forms of production vs. text is to treat Scene; and to consider the use of verbal and nonverbal elements and the ends for which they are used is to deal with Agency and Purpose.

So much for an appropriate vocabulary. A vocabulary alone, however, will not result in criticism. That vocabulary must be used in the processes of description, interpretation, and evaluation.

Description and Interpretation

The first job of the critic is to describe what it is that is being criticized, to identify the critical object with which one is concerned. Such identifications can be lengthy and complex, as when one deals with particular productions and must describe the design elements, acting, directing, script, and the relationships among them, or they can be quite simple, as when the critic is dealing with the importance of a particular scene in a well-known play and need only point out the action of that scene in relation to the rest of the play. This descriptive identification has the important function of showing that the work or part of the work is *there* to be criticized, that it is accessible to other critics and is not something inside the writer's mind or her or his set of values.

In addition to identifying the critical object, the critic must interpret, must make clear the form, the structure that the artist has created. This form may or may not be apparent, and in most of the truly interesting criticism, it is not only not apparent, but its revelation or clarification is a major strength of the criticism. Let me offer two very brief examples.

In Edmond Rostand's *Cyrano de Bergerac*, the protagonist is often played as a poetic figure consumed by his love for Roxane, but though Cyrano is surely a poetic figure, he is considerably more than that. The key to Cyrano is found, I believe, in the duelling scene in Act I, the scene in which he confronts the fop Valvert and composes a ballade as he duels with him. The ability to do those two things simultaneously means that Cyrano is beyond compare as a swordsman and is at least technically gifted as a poet. But that is to say that the duel is not a contest between equals at all. Cyrano, who can make up verse lines while duelling and fit his duel to those lines, is simply toying with Valvert. There are ways in which the duel might end that would thoroughly humiliate Valvert: with Cyrano whipping him out through the theatre; with Cyrano slashing his ribbons to tatters; with Cyrano disarming him and kicking at him as he flees. But Cyrano, the complete master of the situation, carefully constructs his ballade and then deliberately runs his sword through the count. And that tells us a great deal about this protagonist. If the duelling scene is staged properly, it becomes the formal key to the leading character and, in a sense, to the play itself. At its worst, the scene is staged as a duel between equals, one in which the attack is made now by Cyrano, now by Valvert. But that cannot be. Cyrano is using two weapons against his opponent; he employs two Agencies, his sword and the ballade (and it is interesting that the quality of the verse here is considerably above that of the near-doggerel with which Cyrano introduces the cadets in Act II). Were Cyrano to have used his blade alone, clearly he could have dispatched Valvert at once. Thus, while composing a ballade during the duel brings comic tones with it, the duel also shows the cruel side of Cyrano, for he could so easily have "won" and spared his opponent; instead, he announces his intention of killing Valvert, rehearses the killing, as it were, in the refrain of the ballade, and then apparently does just that.[6] Often called a heroic comedy, *Cyrano de Bergerac* is structurally a tragedy, although the protagonist moves in both the tragic and the comic rhythm; in his love for Roxane, there is the beginning, growth, and death of the tragic form, while his duel is part of the fierce, unbending pride that remains the same throughout the play. Cyrano is just a bit like Don Quixote, part romantic dreamer, yes, but heartlessly cruel in his fixed ideas of honor. Of course, this must not be overdone; to play Cyrano as an evil monster is to destroy the entire work; yet to play him simply as romantic gallant is to lose a significant element of the play.

As a second example, consider D. L. Coburn's *The Gin Game,* a work I have mentioned before. I have yet to see a piece of criticism that pointed to what I think is the central element in the formal structure of this play. The script is about two old people in a rest home or nursing home; they meet on the shabby rear porch or patio of the home; the man (Weller Martin) invites the woman (Fonsia Dorsey) to play gin rummy; as they play, the two of them talk, and as they talk, they expose much of the emptiness of their lives, emptiness they each deserve, though they prefer to blame it on luck. Fonsia wins each and every gin game they play; Weller is furious, usually not even trying to hide it; and at the end of the play, Weller raises his cane, lunges toward Fonsia, and slashes downward with all his strength across her chair, just as she dodges upstage. Both the New York production and the script have this action by Weller. That piece of business is the formal key to the play, in my judgment. Unfortunately, the New York production essentially cancelled that closing piece of business with curtain calls in which Hume Cronyn and Jessica Tandy first glowered at each other and then made tentative moves toward the table as if to start another game (and the audience was quick to catch on, for one heard comments like, "Oh, it's O.K., they get together again"). The curtain call business had the extraordinary effect of tending to change the fundamental structure of the play from tragedy to comedy. The gin games played by the two characters constitute an inspired choice by the playwright, for those games deal so directly with the element of chance on which both Fonsia and Weller blame their misfortunes. But the sequence of gin games is structurally a comic device; no matter how upset Weller is, he recovers enough to start another game, and there is always the chance he will win. Until, that is, he attempts to kill or maim Fonsia and then walks slowly indoors. There will be no more gin games; the dramatic action is closed, final, and passional. But then there is that jarringly inappropriate curtain call which starts the whole business over again.

Now, it's a bit odd to say that a single piece of business in a curtain call is central to the form of a work, but I believe that is the case here. It is not that there are no indications before this that Weller and Fonsia take the gin games and, indeed, their entire encounter seriously, for there are. Fonsia, for instance, has complained about Weller as a disturbed personality, with the risk that he might have been sent to a mental hospital. And Weller's every move proclaims the fact that he regards the business of losing at gin as serious. But in the Broadway staging, the performances by Cronyn and Tandy were so skilled, so full of little touches, some humorous, some serious, that one was easily distracted from the reality of this play. And the reality is that this is not at all a piece about two gruff but warm old codgers; the reality is a play about utter loneliness, about two people afraid of, and angry at, the world, and especially about an old man who would rather injure or kill—and that is precisely what Weller's savage attack at the end is designed to do—than to accomodate himself to an actual human relationship. It is one of those endings that makes one understand and rethink the play in retrospect, for it is only at the end that one sees the final curve of the work, the change from the sequence of gin games as a comic device to a series of clashes rising in intensity and culminating in the outburst that ends this episode in Weller's and Fonsia's lives; and it is only at the end that one sees the implication that, in a sense, their very lives are over, for neither will have the opportunity or the desire to establish another truly human contact. It is not a great play, perhaps, but it is a great ending.

All this is part of description and interpretation, the identification of the object of criticism and the drawing out of the form or structure in that object. But these two phases do not make for criticism in any complete sense. What results from description alone is news, information, and we may value such information, especially about plays, performances, and productions of the past. But that is not criticism. What results from description and interpretation together is also information, but information presented from a new perspective, information that allows one to see the play differently, to perceive structure where none was seen before. Some will say that this is part of criticism, that this is at least the beginning of criticism, but I think that even these two stages do not result in criticism proper, for to do criticism, one must describe, interpret, *and* evaluate. To evaluate, standards or criteria must be employed, and the source of those standards, their location, and their use involve important issues in criticsm.

Evaluation

Description, interpretation, and evaluation are part of all criticism. *Dramatic* criticism (as opposed to literary criticism, or rhetorical criticsm, or music criticism, etc.) takes as its objects of concern dramatic texts and/or their realization in performance. Dramatic criticism may deal with texts alone so long as it treats them in dramatic terms, i.e., as works that are performable, but if it does not so treat them, what is being done is literary criticism or some other species of verbal analysis.

In evaluating performed works, dramatic criticism has traditionally sought its standards in the playscript. Roger Gross makes this comment: *"Acting is not good in itself but only as it serves this end of revealing the play as a designed action. The same applies to scene design, music, light, all the elements of the theatrical medium."*[7] This simple statement is, so far as I can judge, representative of attitudes toward performances and the criteria to be used in judging them. Performances are *of* the text, and they are to be considered good, bad, or in between according to standards provided by that text. But if one is evaluating a text apart from any particular performance, critical standards have a different source. Any criticism of a text involves, to some degree, comparison with other texts, for it is impossible to deal meaningfully with a work totally isolated from all other works. Thus, all criticism of texts is, on one level, generic criticism. But that is not to say that textual criticism deals only with, say, tragedy or comedy as categories. Such criticism must also work with the special characteristics of that particular text. Hence, criteria really come from two sources, from the genre to which the text belongs and from the elements that make the work unique within that genre. It would, perhaps, be more accurate to say that critical standards come from the combination of these two sources, from the tension between the ways in which the work conforms to its genre and the ways in which it differs from other members of that genre.

By far the largest part of dramatic criticism is of the above two orders, criticism that evaluates performances in terms of texts or that evaluates texts in terms of their differences from and similarities to other texts. It should be noted that both sorts of criticism treat the text as the object of primary importance, as the item given critical priority.

But there is, or there is coming into being, a third variety of dramatic criticism. Currently, there is a good deal of interest in something called *performance criticism*, interest indicated by the recommendation of the American Theatre Association's Wingspread II Conference that the primary research emphasis for the coming years be placed on performance analysis or performance criticism,[8] by convention panels on the topic,[9] and by statements of journal editors.[10] There are basic questions involved in the very notion of performance criticism: What exactly is it? Does it simply amount to the old business of reviewing that newspaper critics have done for years, reviewing now dignified by a new title?[11] Is it, indeed, possible to do criticism of a performance?

In one sense, there has long been the criticism of performance, for newspaper reviews, textbooks, and scholarly articles have commented on matters of direction, design, and (especially) acting in particular performances of plays. The present interest in performance criticism may well be due to the fact that, as I pointed out above, dramatic criticism has traditionally made the script the object of primary critical importance; specific performances have been ignored or have been judged in terms of the script. In other words, performance has never been the chief object of dramatic criticism, and yet it is the performed work that is the common concern of theatre people.

But can performance be the object of critical concern? What are the alternatives to viewing performance as absent or as secondary to the script? Well, one alternative is to regard performance alone, in its own right, separate and apart from the playscript. While it is not clear that anyone seriously argues for this position, Michael Kirby seems to come close when he writes: "This does not mean that we are opposed to literature, to the scripted play or to playwriting. It merely means that we feel the study of performance itself is, or should be, an independent discipline—one large enough to take the full attention of several journals."[12] However, the idea of performance itself, of "pure" performance, if you will, is problematical. One may describe a great many things about a performance, but as soon as one begins to evaluate, it becomes clear that there is no such thing as the criticism of performance in and of itself. Without going beyond the performance, there can be no criteria on which to build an evaluation. If the text is not considered, that source of critical standards is eliminated, and there is no equivalent of genre in performance (there are general styles of performance that vary from period to period, but these are not logically coherent enough to provide criteria for evaluation). As Gross's comment indicates, the criteria for evaluation ordinarily come from the script, and considered in its own right, a performance is not a performance *of* something, but is simply a performance; as a result, there is no source of criteria for evaluation.

There is another alternative, however; instead of viewing performance as dependent on the text or as an isolated, independent activity, one may regard the text as secondary to the performance. On the face of it, this can seem an implausible notion, but Burke offers a way to make that notion workable (as he has with other seemingly implausible notions). I have said that Burke stresses the flexibility of the terms of the pentad. For example, Scene can mean the stage setting, the period in which the play is written, the physical theatre, etc. And there is a further and vitally important meaning of Scene: in the sense that the text is the usual starting point for performances, in the sense that performance evolves from or grows out of the text, and in the sense that varied (sometimes widely varied) performances have their origins in the same text, Burke's Scene can be used to mean the text, the playscript viewed as the ground, the source of the performances that derive from it. In that sense, Scene (text) contains Act (performance).

Now, in addition to the importance of the ratios between the terms of the pentad, Burke says they are *reversible,* so that Scene can imply Act, and Act can imply Scene.[13] It is just here that performance criticism, as I envisage it, can come into being. As soon as there is the concept of the script (Scene) implying performance (Act), there is also the concept of performance implying the script. The reversibility of the ratios means that the two are inseparable. Thus, performance can be regarded as the corporeal reality that implies the incorporeality of the text,[14] as the visible and material sign of the verbal structure,[15] as the actuality symbolizing the potentiality of the script.[16] In this manner, one may place the primary importance on performance, not performance in isolation nor performance that is secondary to the script, but performance that is logically prior to the written work, that implies that work, and, thus, makes it possible to evaluate by providing the necessary critical standards. To rewrite Gross's statement: A script is not good or bad in itself, but only as it permits performance to reveal it as a designed action.

All this, however, is but assertion. To borrow again from Burke, the only way to demonstrate the value of a particular notion in criticism is to apply it, to show how it works in practice.[17] So, I offer four examples of dramatic criticism: first, a piece of criticism that concentrates on the text as a dramatic structure; second, criticism of a performance in terms of the text performed; and third and fourth, two examples of performance criticism that evaluate texts in terms of performance.

A Midsummer Night's Dream

With *A Midsummer Night's Dream,* the critic should use a somewhat schizophrenic approach, one part of which stresses differences between the characters and emphasizes the comic structure of the play, the other part focusing on similarities between the characters and pointing to elements beyond the comic.

Certainly the most obvious thing to be said is that the characters of this play differ radically. In the simplest terms, there are the mortals and the fairies; as David Young says, "There are two worlds in *A Midsummer Night's Dream*—the kingdom of Theseus and the kingdom of Oberon, the one an orderly society, the other a confusing wilderness."[18] In Burkean terms, there are two principle Scenes in this work. But it quickly becomes evident that this simple distinction is not enough. For instance, the mortals are separable into the members of court and the mechanicals or rustics, and these two groups of characters are in some ways as far apart as are the mortals and the fairies. One may go further: M. E. Comtois finds in the play "four groups of characters—rulers, lovers, fairies, and artisans—each of which has a public function to perform and a private matter to resolve, so that eight patterns of action interweave throughout the play."[19] This view is supported by Young's observation that verse forms in the play function "as a means of characterization," that "although the usage is by no means strict, we associate blank verse with Theseus, Hippolyta, and the courtly world at Athens; couplets with the lovers, especially as they move into the woods; lyrical measures, including song and dance, with the fairyworld; and prose with the mechanicals, despite their attempts at formal verse."[20] From still another vantage point, it can be said that the play is made up of concentric circles: in the inmost circle are the mechanicals, Bottom at their center; then come the lovers, who are not really much better off than the clowns; then Theseus and Hippolyta; then Titania, Oberon, Puck, and the fairies, whose awareness and whose powers extend into all the previous circles; and finally the largest circle, that of the audience.[21] (This last comment may be less relevant to theatre than the others, for it is not immediately clear how these circles would be reflected in a production. But wait.)

On one level, the characters, the Agents of the play and the Scenes they inhabit, are far apart. This view is usually accompanied by the comment that the play deals with the irrationality of love, the lunacy of love; Theseus and Hippolyta are sane and rational beings, but the four lovers behave idiotically, and even Pyramus and Thisbe reflect the ludicrous nature of love. The mortals move back and forth between the worlds of reason and foolishness, between the rational realm of Theseus and the irrational realm of Oberon. And what is passing folly in humans is the norm of behavior for the fairies, who are irresponsible children throughout.[22] In this manner, one can differentiate in various ways between one group of characters and another, and even between one character or group of characters at one stage in the development of the action and that same character or group of characters at a later stage in the action: thus, Theseus and Hippolyta represent the pole of rationality; the mechanicals, especially Bottom, are seemingly sane, but their sanity is sharply simplified or reduced; the four lovers are sane while at court, but in the wood they are ruled by fairies and behave preposterously; and the fairies are thoroughly mischievous and irresponsible.

This emphasis on the differences between characters leads the critic to an emphasis on the play as a comedy, a fantasy, a demonstration of the foolishness of human beings when they are in love. And the play surely is a comedy; the hilarious self-possession of Bottom who recovers from the most amazing blows that fortune directs at him is alone very nearly enough to ensure that designation. But it is not solely Bottom whose behavior defines the play as a comic structure: the lovers, too, meet misfortune, regain their senses, and move on; even Titania and Oberon reflect the same pattern. Chance is king here, at least from the point of view of the mortals, but I will have some comments about a different point of view in just a moment.

The play is a comedy, and it is a comedy of considerable sophistication. That is, outright foolery is involved, but those who treat the play as mere foolery and horseplay miss a great deal. For instance, there are two layers of comedy in Lysander's claim to love rationallly; R. W. Dent comments that "by all conventional Elizabethan standards, tall fair gentle Helena should be the one pursued, and when Lysander boasts his use of reason in preferring a dove to a raven his argument, by those standards, is indeed rational. Our laughter stems from recognizing that it is so only accidentally, as rationalization."[23] Then, Bottom's insistence that the Lion announce his identity may be a sly dig at the Scottish King James VI who was to have his son's baptismal car drawn by a lion, but who put a Moor in the harness instead, "explaining that a lion would scare the ladies."[24] And Titania's line "What angel wakes me from my flow'ry bed?" is reminiscent of Hieronimo's line from *The Spanish Tragedy*, "What outcries pluck me from my naked bed?"[25] Of course, most actual audiences do not catch such references or allusions, yet an awareness of them enriches one's experience of the work. And as always, it is the well-tempered audience that is important; as Young puts it in a comment, part of which I have cited earlier, "If there were only one man in England astute enough to catch the line from Kyd, that man and that line and their interaction merit attention. We must grant the dramatist the same privileges we grant the novelist and the poet—an ideal auditor, reader, or spectator."[26] In other words, the contemporary (virtual) audience appropriate to this play is one of well-read, theatre-wise folk.

A Midsummer Night's Dream is a comedy that is part broad foolery, part clever play of wit. But the play has a serious dimension, odd as that may seem to the casual reader or theatre-goer. Ronald F. Miller points out that recent critics, rather than considering the play frothy, charming, and trivial, have read it as "a study in the epistemology of the imagination."[27] And it is in the process of pointing out likenesses between the characters that one becomes aware of this additional quality of the play.

To begin with a simple instance, the mortals in the play are called Athenians, and some of them have Greek names. But Albert S. G. Canning argues that "in taste and style Theseus and Hippolyta rather resemble rural

English nobility of former times in their love of hunting and promoting popular festivity," and the rustics "are not only thoroughly English in name, style, and occupation, but in their liking for acting and yet ignorance of its rules or management, to some extent may resemble country people living near London in Shakespeare's time."[28] The historical reference to Shakespeare's time aside, this is the kind of observation that is essential to anyone interested in *A Mid Summer Night's Dream* as a work to be performed, for it means that the mortals, as they behave on stage, differ in that they belong to distinctly different classes, but are alike in being quite English.

Then, consider the similarities between the fairy band and the members of the court. Though the fairies may be called childish and irresponsible in some ways, Ernest Schanzer writes, "They are conscientious and very much overworked servants of the queen with little time for idle gossiping"; for example, "in their encounter with Bottom, the tiny fairies, so far from being like children, show themselves accomplished and ceremonious courtiers"; as for Titania and Oberon, "they are the counterpart in the spirit-world of Theseus and Hippolyta, like them full of stateliness and dignity, though more ceremonious and distant. Their quarrel is not a children's squabble,... but a quarrel which, if we are to credit Titania, has been in progress for many months, disrupting the whole body politic of fairyland."[29] This point should not be pressed too much, of course, for the dignity of Oberon dispatching Puck to fetch a magic pansy and of Titania embracing Bottom encumbered with an ass's head must needs be limited. Nevertheless, there are likenesses between fairies and mortals.

I mentioned earlier that the four lovers were sane while at court and irrational in the woods, and though that distinction must be made, there are qualifiers to be added. If inconstancy be a mark of irrationality, then that irrationality began long before the lovers entered the wood. Demetrius deserts Helena before the play begins, and he goes back to Helena for no apparent reason; and though things are sorted out in the end, Dent holds that "love's choices remain inexplicable, and the eventual pairings are determined only by the constancy of Helena and Hermia in their initial inexplicable choices."[30] The mismatching of the lovers is possible because of very scanty characterization, as several critics have observed. Chambers says, "Helena is tall and fair and timid: Hermia is little and dark and shrewish. Demetrius is crabbed and Lysander is languid. It is difficult to say more."[31] This lack of sharp characterization serves an important purpose: as Young puts it, "were they more fully characterized we would develop an interest in and sympathy for them which the pace of the play does not allow."[32] Finally, when the lovers awake from the magic spell, they are supposedly rational, but they describe their experiences as both real and unreal, and they can speak of them only distractedly.[33] Burke would say that the lovers are not always fully Agents, that when ruled by the fairies, it is the Purpose of the fairies that informs the lovers' Acts. Putting all this together, it seems that the simple division between sane-at-court and mad-in-the-wood will not do. There are traces of a kind of madness in the lovers' "sane" love; they themselves do not sharply separate their rational and irrational episodes, and after their dream, they do not describe it as completely dreamlike; and the very thinness of these characters reduces their human status, making them more like the fairies (and the rustics), and allows them to move easily into the spirit world. In brief, the lovers are mortals, but their characters are not sharply split into rational and irrational parts; the two parts inter-mingle throughout the play.

Now to Theseus and Hippolyta, those two pillars of rationality. Shakespeare, of course, drew on (and took his own liberties with) legend for these two figures. Schanzer says that "as far as there is a choice presented in the play it is between two kinds of love, the love of seething brains of the young Athenians, and the more balanced and rational love of Theseus and Hippolyta."[34] But again, this is too simple, too simple and too serious. Hippolyta and Theseus are, of course, the link that holds the plot together; it is their marriage that occasions the festivities, including the performance of *Pyramus and Thisbe;* it is on their wedding day that Hermia's fate is to be decided; it is to celebrate the wedding that the fairies have travelled "from the farthest steep of India." Hippolyta and Theseus are sober figures in many ways, but Theseus was not always so sober; we learn from Titania that he has had various loves. In that same scene between Titania and Oberon, we learn that Hippolyta is Theseus' "buskin'd mistress," "the bouncing Amazon," his "warrior love." And this description fits Oberon's own statement: "Hippolyta, I woo'd thee with my sword,/And won thy love doing thee injuries." Such clues are enough to show these characters in something more than a sombre and rational light. They are big, strong creatures with the strength and the limbs of warriors. And the idea of wooing via swordplay surely provides an element of humor. It would be overdoing it to imagine great-bodied beings flailing away at each other with their swords—slash!—thwack!—crunch!—I think—ouch!—I love you. Overdoing it, certainly. But there is at least a hint of this thumping quality there, and it is enough to lighten the two characters considerably. One can easily imagine a director casting two big, physical types in these parts and then having them, now and then only, bump into someone (or each other) and send that one—not reeling, that would be too much, but tipped off-balance for a second.

There is another point, and a most interesting one, to be noted about Theseus and Hippolyta; it has to do with their attitudes toward the poetic and the fanciful in general and toward the happenings in fairyland in particular. Half way through *Pyramus and Thisbe*, Hippolyta says, "This is the silliest stuff that ever I heard," and Theseus answers, "The best in this kind are but shadows; and the worst are no worse, if imagination amend them." And in his famous opening speech of Act V, Theseus proclaims his disbelief in "these antique fables" and "these fairy toys," and he proceeds to lump together "the lunatic, the lover, and the poet." Dent observes, "In a sense he is obviously right, as Shakespeare never ceases to remind us, but his estimation of such 'shadows' is consistently deprecating."[35] It can seem that Theseus and Hippolyta both show contempt for the world of the imagination. And it is striking that Theseus, this Agent who is himself the product of an antique fable, should so firmly disbelieve such fables and so firmly dispose of the fanciful and the imagined in both love and poetry. But it develops that Hippolyta does not agree with him. She responds to his dismissal of the fairy enchantment ("Or in the night, imagining some fear,/How easy is a bush supposed a bear?") with the discerning lines:

> But all the story of the night told over,
> And all their minds transfigur'd so together,
> More witnesseth than fancy's images,
> And grows to something of great constancy;
> But, howsoever, strange and admirable.

Thumping warriors they both are, yet Hippolyta is willing to grant that something more than a mere trick of the imagination has occurred in the woodland, while Theseus' complete self-assurance is just a bit like Bottom, who is always armored in perfect self-composure.

And it is Bottom, the unlikeliest of creatures, who is the final link in establishing the serious side of *A Midsummer Night's Dream*. E. K. Chambers regards Bottom as "the first of Shakespeare's supreme comic creations, greater than the Costard of *Love's Labour's Lost* or the Launce of *The Two Gentlemen of Verona*, as the masterpiece is greater than the imperfect sketch."[36] Bottom is a dunce, but one who finds nothing in the world strange, one who turns all things to his advantage and does so with sublime self-assurance. And it is via Bottom's role in *Pyramus and Thisbe* and his relationship to the fairies that the play reaches out beyond the sheerly comic vision.

Dent emphasizes the importance of the play within the play. He points out that there is a striking contrast between Shakespeare's play and the mechanicals' drama: Shakespeare has asked the audience to image the moon, to imagine a court, to imagine a fairy realm, yet Bottom and his fellows "can conceive only of real moonshine or a character to 'disfigure' it.''[37] It is as if there were unfettered imagination embodied in Shakespeare's play and its total absence in *Pyramus and Thisbe*. But once more, that is too simple a distinction; there are likenesses to be noted, even here. At the beginning of the rehearsal scene, Bottom asks if everyone is there, Quince says yes, and adds, "Here's a marvail's convenient place for our rehearsal. This green plot shall be our stage, this hawthorn brake our tiring house." But Dent points out that in Shakespeare's theatre there was no green plot, no hawthorn brake. (And Dent might have added that, no matter how realistic the staging, there is never a green plot or a hawthorn brake unless the audience imagine them there.) Hence, what one has is, first, a sharp contrast between the literal-mindedness of Bottom and his comrades and Shakespeare's creative fancy and, next, the presence of Shakespeare's inventive imagination in the previously unimaginative rustics. As a result, there is a sense, as Dent claims, in which the brilliant mingling of the worlds of reality and of the imagination can be seen as "Shakespeare's closest approximation to a 'Defense of Dramatic Poesy' in general.''[38] Again, this point must not be labored, but the odd ties between *A Midsummer Night's Dream* and *Pyramus and Thisbe* should be noted, and they are most clearly seen in the character Bottom.

Bottom's relationship to the fairies is another item of great importance in the play. Puck's speech at the end suggests that the entire play may have been a dream,[39] and that gives rise to one riddle after another: Are the fairies real or unreal? Are the spectators subject to the magic of Puck and Oberon? And Puck's speech is but the last of a long series of clues. The fairies are continuously presented in an indefinite way, largely creatures of a magic world, but also inhabitants of the mortal world: Titania and Oberon rule their own kingdom, but they love Theseus and Hippolyta (who are mysteriously unaware of them); the fairies are completely aware of the mortals as a group and take some delight in complicating the mortals' affairs, yet there is no evil in the fairies, and Puck, for example, is always under Oberon's control, quite as if the underlying attitude toward mortals were a beneficent one. Throughout the play these are hardly pressing issues, but they nag gently at the mind now and then as the work progresses. And it is Bottom who brings the entire matter to a head. We have been prepared bit by bit, for instance with the introduction of the magical aspect of love in Egeus' accusation of Lysander, then by Helena's talk of love transforming reality and Theseus' description of love as a delusion. When the lovers awake from their dream, we know that it is not a dream for we have witnessed the events ourselves. And, of course, along with the act of witnessing the lovers in the forest, we know we are witnessing Shakespeare's play, a play that presents the fairies for our entertainment. But there comes the point when the fictive world of the play shifts, takes on a new dimension. When Bottom, the most literal-minded of humans, meets the fairies, he does not recoil in amazement nor dismiss them (as Theseus might); he simply takes them for granted and sets about talking and making himself at home. Theseus is a rationalist, but Bottom is the realist of the play. He is so simple he thinks the spectators will believe the lion is real unless they are told it is not real, yet he calmly accepts the existence of the fairies, and, as Miller says, his "unblinking acceptance of the fairies provides these metaphoric beings with a solidity that nothing else, not even their presence on stage, can provide."[40] Until their encounter with Bottom, the fairies are presented to us in such a manner as to suggest that they might, somehow, be explained. Were it not for Bottom, the fairies could be regarded as a personification of the providence that, we like to believe, governs affairs.[41] But Miller makes the point that "Bottom is of all men the least prone to the delusions of the imagination, and when he confronts transcendence face-to-face, transcendence itself takes on a certain matter-of-factness."[42] We are struck by the fact that when the lovers awaken, they talk of dream and reality; "they find themselves blessed, but they know not how. Bottom knows, though he finds his language inadequate to describe his 'vision.' "[43] And yet what he does describe is striking in the extreme, though he struggles in the attempt:

> I have had a most rare vision. I have had a dream, past the wit of man to say what dream it was. Man is but an ass, if he go about to expound this dream. Methought I was—there is no man can tell what. Methought I was,—and methought I had,—but man is but a patch'd fool, if he will offer to say what methought I had.

Bottom speaks here in the language of the mystic, admitting humbly the impossibility of recounting his vision. And Bottom *is* a mystic of sorts, for in his blundering, unquestioning fashion he has entered into a realm closed to the other mortals. In so doing, an analogy is established: in Miller's words,

> As Bottom is to the world of the fairies, so man in the height of his powers is to— is to what? If Bottom, the least perceptive of men, can glimpse into the shadowy world of the fairies, what do we who master Bottom's confusions glimpse in our own moments of unarticulated wonder?... A theatrical coup, a witty toying with the levels of reality in the world on stage, comes very close to becoming a parody of mankind caught up in a religious vision of worlds beyond the physical.[44]

And there is something oddly touching, amid the raucous humor, in watching poor Bottom struggle and fail to find the words to express his vision; we pity Bottom in a way, and as Miller says, "the pity is not just for Bottom."[45] But the shift is not completed until we hear Bottom say:

> The eye of man hath not heard, the ear of man hath not seen, man's hand is not able to taste, his tongue to conceive, nor his heart to report what my dream was. I will get Peter Quince to write a ballad of this dream. It shall be called "Bottom's Dream," because it hath no bottom.

Bottom has, of course, echoed St. Paul:

> $_9$But *we preache* as it is written, Things w^c eye hath not sene, & eare hath not heard, nether haue entred into mans mynde, which thinges God hath prepared for the that loue hym. $_{10}$But God hath opened *them* vnto vs by his Sprite, for the Spirite searcheth all things, yea, the botome of Goddes secretes.[46]

And now the extraordinary has happened; Bottom has reached out to that widest circle, the audience, the virtual audience of the ages, and a tie has been established for just a moment between the unreal and fanciful world of the fairies and human faith. "The mysteriousness of the fairies becomes linked with the highest mystery of all. Bottom and St. Paul...."[47]

I have drawn heavily on Miller in describing this tenuous link between Bottom and the issue of human faith. But Dent, too, notes this link: "It used to be customary to see no significance whatever in this echo.... Unlike either the lovers or Bottom, however, we have ourselves been admitted to a more complete vision, though we may well be asses if we seek to infer from it more than the suggestion of a mysterious 'grace' that sometimes blesses true love."[48] And Northrop Frye, in a passing comment, says firmly, "This world of fairies, dreams, disembodied souls, and pastoral lovers may not be a 'real' world, but, if not, there is something equally illusory in the stumbling and blinded follies of the 'normal' world of Theseus' Athens with its idiotic marriage law."[49]

All this must be handled with much care. The play is, after all is said and done, a fantasy, and it cannot really deal with the mystery of faith, for it is not capable of discursive inquiry; nor is a meeting with Titania to be equated with grace. Nevertheless, for just an instant "Bottom's simple-mindedness seems enviable rather than ludicrous, and literalism and faith seem impossible to tell apart."[50] Miller puts its nicely:

> Philosophical distinctions and metaphysical terminology seem absurd before the easy grace of the play, and Pauline discourses on faith seem a far cry from a production full of low comedy and Ovidian fancies. Yet the critic must inevitably risk bringing up such concepts and such discourses if he is to discuss the intellectual complexities of a comedy ending with Puck's suggestion that the play itself may be no more—or less—than another fairy-induced vision.[51]

To put all this on the stage requires the lightest hand, the deftest touch. Most emphatically, Bottom must not be made into a prophet who deals directly with these weighty matters. It is a question of placement, of lighting, of timing, of understanding that the comedy is for a trembling moment quite serious and that the character of Bottom is one of those miraculous theatrical forms that can reach across time and space and human despair and touch the minds of the virtual audience centuries after the play was written.

Bottom is, of course, a major theatrical form, a virtual speaker. But that extraordinary moment of his rests on two minor forms, two forms of mind. First, repetition. Bottom's words are unmistakably a repetition of St. Paul's. A bumbling and garbled repetition, but a repetition. Second, consubstantiality. For most of the play, Bottom is very much *other* to the virtual audience; we observe him, laugh at him, even feel a certain scorn for him; but we are not likely to identify with him. Until, that is, Bottom makes the unforseen move from being a clown to being, if not part of, something close to the virtual audience. Up to that moment, Bottom has very much his own identity, but then, for the briefest instant, he shares our state, he is of our substance. And then, of course, he returns to his separate identity.

At the end of the first chapter, I talked very briefly of theatre as a permanent form of art, and Bottom is a striking instance of that permanency. I have never seen a production of *A Midsummer Night's Dream* which gave the audience a Bottom such as I have described. Thus, I am speaking of a form that I apprehend only in its implicit state. Had I seen, or were I to see, a production with this Bottom, the form would be explicit and would have more impact. But even the implicit form will remain with me for many, many years. For many years and many productions of the play. More important, the form will remain with me when I see other plays in which a character who is seemingly far removed from that outermost circle either gains or might gain membership in that circle for an instant. Like all forms, this one has general applicability. And that is why I am willing to call it permanent. Not permanent in the sense of a statue or a building, but permanent in the sense that it does not depend for its existence on the performance; it comes to full life only in the performance, but it existed (was implicit in the script and in the mind) before the performance, and it exists (is explicit in the mind) after the performance. That sort of existence is, it seems to me, properly called permanent.

I have described two critical processes, tracing the differences and the likenesses between characters; the former leading to a view of the play as a comedy full of humor that is by turns bawdy, gentle, farcical, and witty; the latter to a realization that the play works carefully and subtly toward one great point of serious comedy, with its implication that faith itself is a serious and comic matter.[52] These two processes constitute what is, in my judgment, dramatic criticism, for though they focus on the text, they treat that text in theatrical terms, i.e., as an implicit performance (a virtual performance, if you will). For an evaluation of an actual performance, I turn now to another play.

A Touch of the Poet

The 1978 production of Eugene O'Neill's *A Touch of the Poet* at the Helen Hayes theatre, directed by Jose Quintero, with Jason Robards as Con Melody, Geraldine Fitzgerald as Nora, and Kathryn Walker as Sara,[53] got generally poor reviews. And the reviews more or less agreed on what was wrong with the production, though there were different emphases among them. The major problem was Jason Robards' portrayal of Con Melody. Con is the central character of the play, a self-professed aristocrat who cannot accept either poverty or reality; consumed with resentment at his humble position, he finally sets off to horsewhip the Yankee father who thinks his son is too good for marriage to Con's daughter; he never sees the father, but is clubbed down by the servants and the police and returns to the inn where he discards the *persona* of Major Melody and takes on the *persona* he has fought against all his life, that of Con the Irish peasant. The play is a tragedy solely because of this character and the way he spends himself in efforts destined from the very outset for failure. Walter Kerr says that Robards was convincing in his humiliation and his acceptance of his peasant nature; but before that, Kerr says, Robards gave no hint of being an aristocrat, but was merely "an idle popinjay, tyrant to no purpose"; worse, when he regarded himself in the mirror, priding himself on bearing the stamp of an officer and a gentleman, he simply "bears the stamp of a fop."[54] When he pawed Deborah, the mother of Sara's beloved, the gesture was clumsy enough, "but surely it should have another half to it: some echo of the suave gallantry that must have been his as a young man."[55] Kerr points out that there must be something in the way Con Melody is performed "to justify the lingering admiration his wife and daughter offer his battered ghost in the play's final lines."[56] And the most sweeping complaint Kerr makes is that both Robards' performance and the direction by Quintero fail "to hold in the theatre the poetic impulse"; this impulse must be ever-present, and "those who cling to it may be fools, but they must be ambiguously fools: men with a trace of actual talent, men with color on their tongues, men of ludicrously thwarted aspiration."[57]

John Simon (who avoids his too-frequent vicious excesses in regard to this production) makes similar comments. He says Robards was fine at the end, but unconvincing earlier: "Robards is good at dash, anger, even ruthlessness, but he cannot sustain them as an obbligato while he puts in the lovable blarney."[58] In addition to his lack of charm, Simon says, "One does not believe in [Robards'] military prowess or in his determined rise to specious respectability."[59]

Stanley Kauffman puts it most provocatively. He suggests that one of the interesting things about the play is the link it creates with the theatre of the past. He describes O'Neill, sickened by his father's reliance on such works as *The Count of Monte Cristo*, but coming back in his maturity to the theatre of his father: "talking about the role of Con Melody, [O'Neill] said: 'What that one needs is an actor like Maurice Barrymore (John's father) or James O'Neill, my old man. One of those big-chested, chiseled-mug, romantic old boys.' "[60] One way this play is tied to the past, Kauffman says, is "in O'Neill's reliance on the actor of Melody, as the quotation above proves, to *complete* the play in a way that his other good plays do not so absolutely require."[61] Kauffman believes that the play "does have tragic dimension—the fracture of European romance on American reality—if it has the right actor to give us both sides of the catastrophe."[62] Like the others, Kauffman observes:

> In the last twenty minutes or so of the play, Jason Robards is fine as Melody, on the other side of the catastrophe in which Con is degraded. When the role comes *to* Robards, when he can once again do the one character he can do well—the ironic, self-loathing drunk, the Jamie of *Long Day's Journey* and *A Moon for the Misbegotten*—he fulfills it. But in the major part of the role (pun intended), he is, frankly, appalling.... Instead of a Byron-quoting ex-officer, a fallen emperor with a ragged retinue, we get mugging and caricature."[63]

And the problem, Kauffman claims, is that "Robards (and his director) took the 'elevated' portion of the role as impersonation, a kind of W. C. Fields act of grandeur. Nothing could be falser or more destructive of the play. Either the grand Con is *not* 'acting' or there is no tragedy."[64]

If the reviews are to be believed, the production was weak because Robards and Quintero failed to create a believably ambiguous Con Melody. And some academic critics offer support for the reviewers' verdict in the sense that, working not with a production but with the playscript, they find that the character of Con Melody *is* ambiguous and retains a sympathetic quality, hence is there for the actor to portray. Frederick Carpenter takes the strongest position: "The excellence of the second half of the play lies in the perfect balance between its conflicting characters and motives. Cornelius Melody is always a sympathetic character, because, like most of O'Neill's heroes, he is torn by conflicting inner forces."[65] John Gassner comments: "It is a tribute to O'Neill's power of sympathy that while Con Melody causes us much irritation we can join his rebellious daughter in regretting that he has renounced his pretensions at the end of the play"; and Gassner adds, "O'Neill managed to give Con Melody size as well as vanity. The man has a touch of the poet."[66] Louis Sheaffer writes: "If not for occasional indications of his vulnerability, Con Melody would be totally unsympathetic, especially for his contemptuous attitude toward Nora, who loves him no matter what; but under his lordly posturing he is a sorely beset man."[67] Doris Falk describes the character of Con as part peasant, part aristocrat; "the Irish peasant in Con loves [Nora] in his way, but the Major despises her."[68] And in various ways, other critics agree with this view of Con Melody.[69]

Apparently, then, if Robards' performance was one dimensional, it was Robards' and Quintero's fault, not that of the script. But it is just this issue I want to examine. For this is a typical example of dramatic criticism that evaluates a performance in light of a playscript, and the first thing to do with any such criticism is to see whether or not the critics have understood the script.

Because there is such apparent agreement among critics on the ambiguities built into Con's character by the script, I must try the reader's patience by going through the text and pointing out the times at which Con is clearly ugly, vengeful, or hateful in his treatment of his wife and daughter *and* the times at which there is some tenderness or kindness in his actions.

The first thing to be noted is that, while Con is in permanent conflict within himself, this conflict is not quite as simple as it may seem. We are told by Cregan and Maloy at the beginning of the first act that Con was born in a castle, raised and educated in wealth and in private schools. True, his father had been the keeper of an inn where he sold whiskey illegally, this despite Con's claim that his family was of the gentry. We get Con's background laid out rather laboriously and discursively, and the reasons for, or the specific nature of, the conflict within him are never really made any clearer. It is easy enough to assume that Con has always lived in circumstances in which status was prized and that he never actually possessed that status. But it is important to remember that he was born in wealth, educated in fine schools, and then became an officer in the army. Son of a peasant, yes; a peasant himself, now or in the past, no.

Beyond this general point, there are a good many specifics that are of importance. In Act I, the stage directions describing Con's first entrance state that Con sees Sara, the two look at each other, she turns away in scorn and hostility, and for just a moment Con "looks guilty," but quickly recovers. This is the first hint of any duality of character. The stage directions go on to describe Con as having the manner of "a polished gentleman," but overdoing it, "overplaying a role which has become more real than his real self to him."[70] After some cold remarks to his wife, he allows or entices Nora to suggest that he have a drink, then when he has the liquor in front of him bursts out and accuses her of deliberately encouraging his drunkenness, saying it is the only way she can be superior to him. Then, for a second he is sorry; he says, "Forgive me, Nora. That was unpardonable," and the stage directions indicate that he is guilty for a moment and shows tenderness and affection. A few lines later, Con remembers that it is the anniversary of his moment of glory at Talavera; preparing to get out his old uniform for him to wear, Nora tells him he is so handsome in it that "no woman could take her eyes off you." Con boasts, "But it's true, in those days in Portugal and Spain—." He stops shamefacedly, accordingly to the stage directions, then when Nora is not offended at his reference to other women, Con says, "You have the kindest heart in the world Nora," and the stage directions say his voice breaks. But he immediately changes mood, and a few speeches later refers to the Irish problem, adding at once, "But why do I discuss such things with you?" Nora humbly admits her ignorance, and Con says, "Yes I tried my best to educate you, after we came to America—until I saw it was hopeless." Nora continues in her humble vein, "You did, surely. And I tried, too, but—." And Con goes on, "You won't even cure yourself of that damned peasant's brogue. And your daughter is becoming as bad." Two lines later, in what may be the only *unprompted* words of kindness in the first three acts, Con says, "I owe you an apology for what happened last night." Nora replies, "Don't think of it." Con says he'd had a bit too much too drink and goes on, "I'm afraid I may have— The thought of old times— I become bitter. But you understand, it was the liquor talking, if I said anything to wound you." Nora answers, "I know." And Con responds, "You're a sweet, kind woman, Nora—too kind." The stage directions say he embraces her and kisses her. But then he pushes her away in revulsion and disgust, saying, "For God's sake, why don't you wash your hair? It turns my stomach with its stink of onions and stew!" Nora recoils as if struck, and says, "I do be washin' it often to plaze you. But when you're standin' over the stove all day, you can't help—." (Kerr gets this wrong; he says Con repulses Nora "because she hasn't washed her hair."[71]) Con says, "Forgive me, Nora. Forget I said that. My nerves are on edge. You'd better leave me alone." Nora goes out to fix his breakfast, Con moves down in front of the mirror and preens before it, quoting lines from Byron; Sara comes in and sees him, and there is an angry scene between the two of them, followed by the entry of Roche, O'Dowd, and Riley, Con's camp followers, as it were. Then, at the end of the act, Nora brings in Con's breakfast and says, "Con! Have this in your stomach first! It'll all get cauld." Con: "(without turning to her— in his condescendingly polite tone) I find that I am not the least hungry,

Nora. I regret your having gone to so much trouble." He goes into the bar, and Nora sinks down at the table and sobs quietly.

At the beginning of Act II, Con comes in from the bar, sits down and for a moment continues the Byronic pose, but the stage directions say that without an audience he cannot maintain the fiction, and he sags in hopelessness and defeat. Sara enters; she attacks him for forcing her to beg for credit and for treating her mother like a slave. Con attacks in turn, suggesting that she will need to trap her young man with sex; his key lines are, "Faith, the poor young devil hasn't a chance to escape with you two scheming peasants laying snares to trap him," and, "And if all other tricks fail, there's always one last trick to get him through his honor!" Sara leaves, and Con protests to Nora that his daughter has misunderstood him. Nora says its alright, that she understands that Con is remembering her own sin with him. At which Con exclaims that it wasn't Nora who seduced him, but the other way round. And he adds: "And how about you in those days? Weren't you the prettiest girl in all Ireland? (scornfully) And be damned to your lying pious shame! You had no shame then, I remember. It was love and joy and glory in you and you were proud!" These are the strongest lines in the first three acts insofar as Con's love for Nora is concerned; they strongly affirm Cregan's statement at the beginning of Act I to the effect that Con may choose now to say that he had to marry Nora because she was pregnant, but that, as Cregan puts it, "He married her because he'd fallen in love with her, but he was ashamed of her in his pride at the same time because her folks were only ignorant peasants on his estate, as poor as poor." (Kerr gets this wrong, too; he says Con married "only because a child was coming."[72])

Act III. It is evening, and Con is celebrating with Jamie Cregan, his old companion in arms, and the three drinkers, O'Dowd, Roche, and Riley. Sara is trying to clean up after a long day of work. In front of the others, Con says he must apologize for the service, that "the waitress" has not been able to learn her job properly. Then, in another long confrontation with Sara, Con asks if she is jealous of his mare because "she has such slender ankles and dainty feet?" He follows this with, "Keep your thick wrists and ugly, peasant paws off the table in my presence, if you please! They turn my stomach! I advise you never to let Simon get a good look at them—." Sara is shocked and shamed. Con is briefly guilty: "Forgive me, Sara. I didn't mean—the whiskey talking—as you said." He goes on, "An absurd taunt, when you really have such pretty hands and feet, my dear." But then he continues his attack. He says he has talked to young Harford, Sara's young man, has forced him to promise to marry Sara to protect her good name; but he adds that he agrees with Harford's mother, who wanted him to wait a year. Sara is distraught at hearing this.

Con goes on and on and finally says he has decided to oppose the marriage. The important lines are these: "Well, to be brutally frank, my dear, all I can see in you is a common, greedy, scheming, cunning peasant girl, whose only thought is money and who has shamelessly thrown herself at a young man's head because his family happens to possess a little wealth and position"; "So, I have about made up my mind to decline for you Simon Harford's request for your hand in marriage"; "As a gentleman, I feel I have a duty, in honor, to Simon. Such a marriage would be a tragic misalliance for him—and God knows I know the sordid tragedy of such a union"; "I hold young Harford in too high esteem. I cannot stand by and let him commit himself irrevocably to what could only bring him disgust and bitterness, and ruin to all his dreams"; "You are pretty. So was your mother pretty once. But marriage is another matter. The man who would be the ideal husband for you, from a standpoint of conduct and character, is Mickey Maloy, my bartender, and I will be happy to give him my parental blessing—"; "You and he could be congenial. You can match tongues together. He's a healthy animal. He can give you a raft of peasant brats to squeal and fight with the pigs on the mud floor of your hovel." After this devastating assault on his daughter, and after Sara leaves the room, Con starts to go out, then stops; he crumbles for a moment, "Sara! There are things I said which I regret—even now. I—I trust you will overlook— As your mother knows, it's the liquor talking, not— I must admit that, due to my celebrating the anniversary, my brain is a bit addled by whiskey—as you said." But Sara has not heard any of it. And Con turns to his mirror again for comfort. Then, near the end of the act, Con has decided to confront the senior Harford and to challenge him to a duel for refusing Sara as a wife for young Simon. Sara knows very well that Mr. Harford will not even see Con, but when she begs him not to go, Con shouts, "You'd sell your pride as my daughter—! (his face convulsed by fury) You filthy peasant slut! You whore! I'll see you dead first—! By the living God, I'd kill you myself! (He makes a threatening move toward her)." Cregan intervenes, and Con goes out to seek his duel.

In Act IV, there is only one instance of Con's ugliness. Sara admits that she and Simon have been to bed, and though Con (now the peasant) first says in his brogue that he is glad, he continues in this fashion: "Be the living God, it's me should be proud this night that one av the Yankee gintry has stooped to be seduced by my slut av a daughter! (Still keeping his eyes fixed on hers, he begins to rise from his chair, his right hand groping along the table top until it clutches the dueling pistol. He aims it at Sara's heart, like an automaton, his eyes as cold, deadly, and merciless as they must have been in his duels of long ago. Sara is terrified but she stands unflinchingly.)" In the rest of the act, Con is the Irish peasant who, at least in his own way, loves his wife and daughter. And his love is now open and unmistakable. He tells Nora he loves her, he kisses her hair, and he tells her to pay no attention to the things "the Major" said.

There is, of course, a vast amount I have not mentioned, but I have listed these specifics because, if I am to argue that the critics are wrong about this play and the 1978 production, it seems to me necessary to have the evidence laid out clearly. And I believe the critics are wrong.

One of the first things to notice is that many of the ambiguities in Con's character are indicated in stage directions only. That is, they are not part of the dialogue to be enacted, but are discursive statements by the author. Indeed, stage directions are the author's comments on the artwork, and, as such, they take their place beside the observations of other critics. And O'Neill may well be an indifferent critic of O'Neill.[73] Further, one must keep in mind Hernadi's point that the logic of the matter forces one to regard the finished product as either the performed work or the verbal artifact (stage directions included); my own argument in favor of the former has already been advanced. Thus, stage directions, while not to be disregarded automatically, carry with them no presumption of dramatic truth, or even of importance, in regard to the theatrical event.

Beyond that general point, some of these stage directions, e.g., the description of Con as a polished gentleman, are tied to no specific dialogue or stage business. And many of those that are descriptions of particular actions or line-readings, e.g., those about Con's entrances, are difficult, if not impossible, to observe. To have had Robards stop, look at Sara, then show guilt would very likely have slowed down Con's initial entrance in an undesirable way; and to have followed all such directions would surely have made for unfortunate pieces of dead stage time. It is not that Robards ignored such authorial comments, but simply that, in order to keep the tempo of the performance alive, he could not make them anything but fleeting moments, moments that in over-all terms have little impact and reveal no significant amount of conflict in Con's character.

Then there is the sheer difference in the weight and the quality of the kindnesses and the hurts that Con dispenses. There are points at which Con is warm, even loving, to Nora in the first three acts, but there is a twofold problem with these moments. First, they are too frequently followed by additional ugly words, as when Con pushes her away, repulsed by the smell of cooking. Second, and more important, they are tiny in comparison to the violent outbursts of rage. He heaps on his wife abuse that far exceeds what one thinks of as appropriate limits, even for one in the midst of conflict. With Sara, the case is even clearer. When he calls her a slut, mocks her thick wrists, and even threatens to kill her, it is no longer a question of a simple imbalance between tenderness and cruelty; the entire issue of balance has disappeared. Con has so far transcended the boundaries of decency that there is no possibility of taking back or making up for what he has done. Unkindness is one thing, viciousness and savagery another.

Finally, there is the terrible fact that Con feels he has a right to abuse Nora and Sara as a matter of course. One might understand his lashing out in the middle of an argument, but his insults often come for no reason at all, e.g., saying Sara was a waitress who hadn't learned her trade (this in front of the hangers on who knew quite well who Sara was) and boasting of other women he had had to Nora.

Insofar as the conflict or ambivalence in Con Melody is reflected in his attitudes and actions toward his wife and daughter, matters are so one-sided that, for the first three acts of the play, Con has pitifully few redeeming moments. But to put it that way is to raise an important question. *Is* the ambivalance in Con reflected in his behavior toward Nora and Sara? After all, he has important scenes with Cregan, Maloy, Roche, O'Dowd, and Riley, and with the lawyer from Mr. Harford. And the question is made more pressing by the comments of the reviewers: Kauffman, Kerr, and Simon all complain that Robards should have been more believable as an officer, a conquering soldier, a fallen emperor. Perhaps the conflict in Con is not to be found in the cruelties and kindnesses shown to Nora and Sara, but in the contrast between military commander and humble peasant.

The critics are correct, I believe, in that Robards was not convincing as the great military hero. Even the photographs in the playbill show him as a stoop-shouldered man, anything but the fallen emperor. But if the conflict is one between a military hero and a peasant, then this play is doomed from the start. Either a military hero or a peasant might be consistently tender or consistently abusive toward wife and daughter, and if either behavior occurs consistently, there is little conflict to be seen in the character. In addition, the Scene in which Con operates for most of the play, and for most of the important parts of the play, is not a battlefield, not a military setting, but the humble inn where he lives with his wife and daughter. There are scenes with other characters, to be sure, but it is to Nora and Sara that he reveals himself fully. And the scenes with Nora and Sara can hardly show the divided nature Con fights against if the division is simply between officer and peasant. They can show that nature only if it is a conflict, a division between father/husband/officer and father/husband/peasant. The Acts given this Agent, the Acts most important to the play, are the Acts of a husband and father. Thus, if there is to be conflict, it must be shown in the roles of husband and father. And it is just there, in those roles, that the actor is given the least to work with, despite O'Neill's dependence on the actor to complete his play. I think the critics were wrong to blame Robards for not showing us the ambiguities of Con's character, for the problem is not in the performance but in the script; and it is a problem that is deeply rooted enough to make me doubt that any actor could do much more than Robards did, for the words and actions are simply not there to be used. It is almost as if the critics were treating the play as literature rather than as theatre. One can read *A Touch of the Poet* and imagine various things into the text, including a profound conflict in Con Melody, a conflict shown in various ways. But if one reads the play as a theatre piece and considers what an actor can do on stage, one finds almost constant hostility, ugliness, and cruelty in Con's behavior.

All this is not to say that the production was free of problems. Far from it. Though it had strengths that were many and important, the production was seriously flawed. The simplest flaw was the placement of the mirror at extreme downstage left, so that Con preened himself and recited Byron looking off into the wings. The most complicated weakness was the speech used by the actors (so often a problem in the American theatre). John Henry Raleigh describes the significance of the Irish brogue in the play, especially as a weapon between Con and Sara.[74] The brogue is important, indeed, but it was handled poorly in this production by Robards; his diction was phonetically inconsistent, particularly when compared to that of Geraldine Fitzgerald and, to a lesser degree, Kathryn Walker. Worse, throughout the first three acts, Robards and Walker (when she was not lapsing into brogue) used General American speech. This is a poor choice for Con; as the would-be aristocrat and the hater of Americans, he would surely speak in Standard Southern British diction (though the choice of an upper class Irish accent would be interesting). Robards, never an actor with strong technique, spoke in this production exactly the same way he did in *A Moon for the Misbegotten* and even in his film work.

Another problem with the production was that little was done to cover up the excessive amount of discourse in the play. Falk observes that "every action is explained by the characters.... O'Neill is not satisfied with having Con act out his ridiculous and pathetic illusions, but must always make him analyze them.... [Nora], too, analyzes herself for the audience."[75] This sort of thing poses a terrible problem for director and actors; if the actors simply sit or stand and talk, the discursive form is emphasized (and that is what happened in this production), and if various kinds of stage business are inserted, there is the risk of having the business seem added on, seem extraneous to the dramatic action of the play. Quintero apparently chose to avoid the second evil, and, as a result, fell prey to the first.

There were problems with the production, though many of them originated in the script. But there was one major strength in the production, and one that did *not* spring from the playscript. Geraldine Fitzgerald gave an extraordinary performance. Kerr damns her with faint praise, saying, "Of the others, Miss Fitzgerald fares best."[76] Simon does exactly the same thing: "As Nora, Geraldine Fitzgerald satisfies."[77] Only Kauffman prizes Fitzgerald's work: "The treasure of the evening is Geraldine Fitzgerald as Nora, Con's patient, devoted wife.... Her Nora is rich, peasant-wise, enduring, and endearing."[78] But even Kauffman gives no hint as to the importance of the part or the difficulty that Fitzgerald faced as a performer. Most of O'Neill's women are problem parts: as Sheaffer says, "O'Neill created in the majority of his leading female characters either bitches and other agents of misfortune or impossibly noble souls. He could praise Woman only in exaggerated, unrealistic terms."[79] As for Nora, Falk comments that she "is a forgiving and browbeaten Earth-Mother, who while pitiable is still a little sickening in her mooning over the handsome husband who has spent his life abusing her."[80] And Sheaffer observes, "As for Nora Melody, prematurely aged from worry and overwork, the author has idealized her into a household saint in broken-down brogans."[81] It was apparently no accident that O'Neill wrote this sort of character; many writers have noted his inability to deal with women in his plays,[82] and in regard to the film *Odd Man Out*, in which the heroine dies to save her lover, O'Neill is said to have remarked, "That's how it should be. When a woman loves a man, she should be prepared even to give her life for him."[83]

How shall an actor deal with this character in such a way as to avoid the trap of the whining, pitiful, and sickening character that seems all too ready to spring from the script? It is an important instance of the production having to repair the script. I have no idea what Fitzgerald (or Quintero) thought about, talked about, or decided to do. But Geraldine Fitzgerald somehow gave Nora strength, and not simply the so-called strength of the meek and submissive. She spoke often with vigor and animation, and in that terrible moment when Con had pushed her away and asked why she didn't wash her hair, she was filled with pain, but answered in a direct manner, not angrily, but firmly and in a way that objected to Con's unwarranted insult. Fitzgerald managed, in that line-reading and throughout, to find a magic balance between submission and a sense of the character's worth. I remember thinking at one point in the performance that she had, in some fashion, created the impression of a background, a culture of her own that was to be preserved.

It is instructive to compare Fitzgerald's performance with that of Helen Hayes, who played Nora in the original Broadway production. Gassner says, "Miss Hayes appeared too consciously an actress in her part."[84] Robert Brustein is far more blunt:

> I can think of no reason, apart from Mr. Clurman's theory of the play, why Helen Hayes should have been permitted to superimpose Mrs. McThing on the part of Melody's wife; she gives the impression, through ingratiating gestures, mischievous inflections, and a waddling gait, of a star determined to compensate for the ignominy of a non-stellar role by having an extra-dramatic love affair with every member of the audience.[85]

Nothing could be further from the artistry that Fitzgerald brought to the play.

The actor who plays Con Melody faces an absolutely impossible task, in my judgment; the best he can do is to fail admirably. Jason Robards' performance was by no means the definitive one, but he is not to be blamed for problems in the script that cannot be covered up. The actor who plays Nora Melody faces a monumentally difficult task, for she must find ways to hide flaws in the text without openly violating that text. Geraldine Fitzgerald found (and not in the script) a way to turn Nora into a believable woman who was not merely a servile drudge. She deserves great praise for her work.

Thus, the evaluation of the performance in terms of the script was not, in my belief, aptly done. There are standards implicit in the script that can be used to judge the performance, but both reviewers and academic critics seem to have strayed far from the text; some of them appear to have begun with the performance and then to have imagined a better and more satisfying performance, without realizing that the script does not support that preferred performance. It is as if they were working with a virtual text and ignoring the actual one; the one which does not give Robards the tools to do what they expect of him and, perhaps more important, does not give Fitzgerald the tools to do what she, in fact, did and what they too nearly overlooked.

I have now presented two examples of dramatic criticism, the first of a playscript, the second of a production. Most dramatic criticism is of these two types. But just above I have raised the issue of actors covering up weaknesses in scripts, of actors improving on scripts. And that issue, along with others closely related to it, I want to explore in the following two examples of performance criticism. The first one deals with performance matters similar to Fitzgerald's work, the second with more complex questions.

Equus

In the New York production of *Equus*,[86] the part of Martin Dysart, the psychiatrist, was played by several different actors. Typically, one would evaluate the work of these actors in relation to the script, but, following my earlier argument, I propose to reverse matters here and to judge the script in terms of the acting that was done.

Throughout the play, there is a concept of *passion* that is central to everything that happens. The boy blinds the horses, not simply because he is bad, but because he is the prisoner of a passion that is partly sexual, partly religious. The psychiatrist becomes involved with the boy, envies the passionate creature that he is, and bemoans his own lack of passion. The boy's mother says with her own passion that one is responsible for one's acts, and the boy's father carries the guilt of his secret passion. Even the magistrate who sends the boy to the psychiatrist is passionately dedicated to helping the helpless. And key scenes in the play involve the passion (or lack of it) that exists between the boy and the girl and the boy and the noble horse.

The notion of passion is at the very core of *Equus*, and it is this notion that creates a paradox in the play, a paradox expressed clearly in this speech by the psychiatrist:

> I tell everyone Margaret's the puritan, I'm the pagan. Some pagan! Such wild returns I make to the womb of civilization. Three weeks a year in the Mediterranean, every bed booked in advance, every meal paid for by vouchers; cautious jaunts in hired Fiats, suitcase crammed with Kao-Pectate! Such a fantastic surrender to the primitive! And I use that word endlessly: *"primitive."* "Oh, the primitive world," I say. "What instinctive truths were lost with it!" And while I sit there, baiting a poor unimaginative woman with the *word* that freaky boy tries to conjure the *reality!* I sit looking at pages of centaurs trampling the soil of Argos—and outside my window he is trying to *become one,* in a Hampshire field! . . . I watch that woman knitting, night after night— a woman I haven't *kissed* in six years—and he stands in the dark for an hour, sucking the sweat off his God's hairy cheek.[87]

Richard Burton played the role of the psychiatrist in a very intact fashion, i.e., with verbal and physical behaviors that were congruent, and he made of this speech (and others) an unmistakable outburst of passion. When he did, the central weakness of the play became clear. The speech is an outcry against the character's passionless state; but if the actor cries out passionately, he contradicts himself; and if he speaks dispassionately, he is not crying out. It is the dramatic equivalent of the classic paradox of the liar. And the paradox is by no means limited to some key speeches of the psychiatrist. As a passionate and compassionate being, the psychiatrist might well understand the boy's sickness, but he would be unlikely to find it attractive, as he does; as a passionless, lonely figure, he might envy the boy, but he would be unable to create the close relationship with him that he finally builds. Thus, it is not only his attitude toward himself, but also his relationship with the boy (and, hence, the plot of the play) that is dependent on the psychiatrist's passionate or passionless character. How to enact this paradox!

Anthony Hopkins had earlier solved the problem. He acted the part in an oddly disjointed fashion. His physical behavior was relaxed, almost limp at times, while his verbal behavior was energetic, often highly charged. When he uttered the lines quoted above, his face and body showed little emotion, but his voice was vibrant with pain. And so he found a way out of the dilemma: vocally and verbally, he made a passionate statement; physically, he was the passionless being he claimed to be. (And if there be any doubt that these acting techniques were deliberately chosen, one has but to watch Hopkins' performance of Othello in the BBC Shakespeare series. It is a performance with no trace of the disjointedness of his work in *Equus*.)

In the one case, the acting (Hopkins') concealed the contradictions built into the script; in the other, the acting (Burton's) demonstrated those contradictions, thereby providing a basis for evaluating the script. I must emphasize that performance criticism, as I am describing it, does not call for the critic to simply label one performance bad, the other good. Hopkins' performance served the play well; evaluated in terms of the script, it was the better performance, for it helped to make convincing a work with quite serious flaws. Burton's performance disclosed the play to us; if the text is evaluated in terms of the performance, his was the better job, for it helped us see clearly the structure of the work being performed. As I envisage it, the performance critic's task is to point out the nature of each performance and to show how one can be evaluated in terms of the play while the other offers criteria in terms of which the play can be evaluated.[88]

A Piece of Monologue

I turn now to a much more complicated example, one in which I shall try to show how a particular performance can be used, not only to evaluate the work performed, but also to demonstrate what is required for a work to be performable, i.e., theatrical.

Samuel Beckett's *A Piece of Monologue* is a short, one-character play. The script was published in *The Kenyon Review*, Summer 1979, and the play had its world premier at La Mama Etc in New York on December 14, 1979.[89] In terms of both the script and the performance, this is Beckett's most spare, most minimal work so far (at the time of this writing, that is), and I shall have more to say on that point later. First, I want to evaluate the performance in terms of the text, then the text in terms of the performance.

Watching *A Piece of Monologue*, the audience faced a small, completely black-draped, false proscenium stage. When the curtains parted, one saw an actor in a white wig, a white gown, and white socks standing downstage right; downstage center was a white globe light on a column; and downstage left there was the wooden foot of a bed. That is all one saw throughout the play. I say "saw," but it was not easy or ordinary seeing. The only light came from the white globe, and while the wig and the gown reflected light and were visible, the actor's face was a dim shadow. No features, no character quality, not even the movement of his lips could be seen. The black drapes, of course, hungrily swallowed every ray of light.

The actor spoke in a low-pitched voice at very low volume, but the voice was amplified so that the words were easily understood. A strangely impersonal quality resulted from the amplification, from the unvaried line-readings used, and from the inability to see lip movements. One could not tell whether the actor was speaking or the voice was recorded. There was not the tiniest hint of a fluff of any sort, of a mispronunciation or slurred syllable, and this added to the mechanical effect.[90]

The actor uttered words and phrases, very rarely a sentence. The script consists of 424 fragments of speech, most of them innocent of syntax. These fragments make up a mosaic that pictures cloudily the past and present existence of an old man who has led an empty life and who faces a meaningless death. There are few specifics given, however, and the description I have just offered is very largely inferential. Perhaps the most obvious thing about the script is its highly repetitive nature. Over and over, there are references to loved ones, to getting up at nightfall, to striking matches in order to light a lamp, to facing a wall, to parted lips that begin to speak, to an unknown source of light, to staring out at darkness or emptiness. In addition, the terms "fade" and "frame" are repeatedly used in a cinematic sense. These repetitions slowly give a vague picture of a pointless life that has dwindled to this single room; apparently, the inhabitant has no friends or relatives; his parents are dead, and even their pictures have been taken down and torn up; he exists in his room as if it were an alien land, and he stares out of the window or at a blank wall, indifferent as to which is which.

The monologue is in the third person. The pronouns, he, his, and him occur twenty-nine times, although most of the verbal fragments lack subjects. Also, the word-groups regularly have the verb in the third person, "gropes," "strikes," "takes off," "holds," etc. The character, named Speaker in the script, is describing someone; that someone is not another person, but is the Speaker himself, a fact that makes the work reflexive in nature. The Speaker describes the clothes he wears, his hair, his fixed stare into the dark, and all in the third person. The work is, thus, self-referential, which means that the Speaker, as he performs, is both describing and enacting, and this duality of function ties the performance directly to the script. The Speaker repeatedly describes himself as staring out into the dark ("staring" is used twelve times), and throughout the monologue he stands motionless and stares, save for two slight movements, two twists of the upper body toward stage right. The many mentions of darkness and the lack of light are matched by the very dimly lit stage. And the repetition, the fragments heard again and again in unvaried line-readings, give appropriate expression to the pointlessness of existence. The mechanical-sounding voice removes any trace of life or vitality that might be left in the text. In other words, the form of the script and the form of the production match perfectly; indeed, they are fused into one, and it is almost impossible to tell when one is talking of the script, when of the performance. This point is especially important because it means that there is far less flexibility than usual here, far less opportunity for calculated disagreement between the script and the production (as in the case of Hopkins' performance, or Fitzgerald's). Because the two forms match, one may say that the performance clearly and accurately reveals the structure of the play. In Burke's terms, the Act contains and implies the Scene. As evaluated in terms of the text, the performance works and is quite successful.

But now let me reverse matters and look at the script in terms of the performance. The audience saw a figure whose face was largely invisible, a figure standing on a stage so dimly lit that the eye kept returning to the one source of light, the globe downstage center. When looking at any other object, one strained without success; no clear outlines could be seen. As a result, the eyes lost focus, and one sank into an empty stare; when combined with the bodiless voice that droned its fragments of speech on and on, the result was intensely soporific. Many audience-members stared at the globe in a self-mesmerizing fashion, and one noted the efforts to stay awake, the shifting, pinching oneself, etc. Ordinarily, one would consider such audience behavior a clue to some weakness in the performance, but that was not the case here. Though this was a performance without movement, without vocal variety, without narrative line, without a face on which to center one's attention, without a recognizably live voice to hear, in terms of the script, this empty, almost lifeless performance was entirely apposite, for the script is similarly empty and the performance makes full disclosure of that emptiness. In addition, the performance tells us something about theatre itself. In recent years, Beckett has experimented with pieces that have pared away more and more of what he clearly sees as nonessentials. But until *Monologue,* he nearly always had certain theatrical devices at his disposal: the pacing and the offstage voice in *Footfalls,* the three voices in *That Time,* the three characters and the spotlight that snapped back and forth between them in *Play.*[91] But here there is very little indeed. Too little, I think, for theatre to exist. I make no claims about minimal levels in other arts—and, in fact, it may even be the case that *Monologue* works as a piece of literature—, but theatre involves certain indispensable elements. One must know that what one sees and hears is theatre, that one is attending a live performance.[92] This is just the reverse of the issue of the audience discussed in the first chapter; it is not the live audience, but live performers that make for theatre. One must have something on which visual attention can be centered, and the actor's face is the natural focus of the audience's gaze. In *Monologue*, the actor's face was virtually invisible, there was no movement to observe, and one could not even tell that the actor was actually speaking.[93] The result was that one heard words, and that was about all. But words alone do not make theatre.

Of course, one may ask whether or not *this* performance is the proper basis for an evaluation of *Monologue*. That is, might it not be the case that, as with *Equus*, a performance somewhat at odds with the script would hide some of its flaws and make for a better piece of theatre? One answer has already been given: because of the reflexive dimension of this work, the performance and the text are tied tightly together, and very little room is left for innovative staging; one has only to imagine energetic and varied line-readings, or the sharply lit face of the Speaker, or impatient movements back and forth to understand how quickly such devices would destroy the emptiness and deadness demanded by the script. A second answer is closely related to the first: this is one of the clearest examples of similarity between the direct and reverse functions of signs, images, and symbols; in fact, for much of the work, the words, shapes, and colors of the play appear to have *synonymous* direct and reverse functions. Still another answer is provided by Burke. He uses the phrase "representative anecdote"[94] to refer to the process of reducing a complex whole to a part that still captures the essence of the whole. Drama is the representative anecdote he chooses to stand for the whole of human motivation. Similarly, a playscript, with all the possible productions and performances that script implies, can be reduced to a single performance if, and only if, that performance is properly representative of the script. What is wanted, Burke says, is the kind of reduction of whole to part that is synecdochic and not metonymic,[95] that is, the kind that retains the essential qualities of the whole rather than reducing them to a part that is physical or material. The performance of *A Piece of Monologue* I have described is just such a representative anecdote, and as a synecdoche for the script, the performance makes manifest the nature and limitations of that script. More important, when the script as an implicitly theatrical work is reduced to this explicit performance, the result is a demonstrable absence of those elements essential to theatre.

In addition, this performance reveals neither tragic nor comic form in the work. By comparison with the comic form of *A Midsummer Night's Dream* with its serious dimension, the tragic form of *A Touch of the Poet* based on the struggle and "death" of the Major, the tragic form of *Equus* built on the death-bound career of Dysart (and even the comic form of "How Do I Love Thee" and the tragic form of "Annabel Lee"), there is in *A Piece of Monologue* neither the recovery from the blows of fortune that reflects the vitality of comedy nor the growth, maturation, and decline of the protagonist's character that is the sign of tragedy. *Monologue* comes closer to the form of literature than to that of drama, closer to the creation of virtual life or experience in the mode of memory, for though the Speaker enacts as he describes, his actions are largely directed toward the past (the literary mode) rather than leading inevitably to a future (the mode of drama).

Unlike the paradox that Hopkins' performance resolved in *Equus*, Beckett has here involved himself in a massive paradox for which there is, in my judgment, no resolution, for there is no such thing as untheatrical theatre. From Aristotle to Grotowski, we have heard condemned or declared dispensable that which is sheerly theatrical. And while it is true that the use of theatrical devices constitutes a remarkably flexible aspect of theatre, there comes a point at which we must have the *theatrical* if we are to have *theatre* at all.[96] Without the actor's living voice and body, without lighting that directs the eye of the viewer, without verbal and nonverbal action that begins, develops, and ends, without all these one has something, perhaps, but not theatre. And *A Piece of Monologue* lacks very nearly all of these.

Hence, this *is* the proper performance in terms of which to evaluate this play, for the performance discloses sharply the power of the paradox Beckett has invoked.[92] In terms of the script, the performance is exceedingly well done; the almost unseen Speaker's face and the mechanical-sounding voice are brilliant touches that capture the essence of the script. But at the same time, these imaginative touches demonstrate that the paradox has no resolution within the confines of the art of theatre. This performance, then, has critical importance for *A Piece of Monologue* and for theatre itself.

If my arguments regarding *Equus* and *A Piece of Monologue* hold, this sort of performance criticism has a place in theatre studies. It is not at all a question of doing away with conventional criticism, merely of reversing our critical priorities at times and using selected performances as critical standards by which to demonstrate the strengths and weaknesses of the works performed and to test the limits of the art of theatre.

Notes

[1] Among the best descriptions of the critical process with which I am familiar are: Northrop Frye, *Anatomy of Criticism* (New York: Antheneum, 1967), pp. 3-29; Frye, *The Critical Path: An Essay on the Social Context of Literary Criticism* (Bloomington: Indiana University Press, 1971), especially ch. 1; R.S. Crane, *Critical and Historical Principles of Literary History* (Chicago: University of Chicago Press, 1967), pp. 13-17; Crane, *The Languages of Criticism and the Structure of Poetry* (Toronto: University of Toronto Press, 1953), especially pp. xi-xvi; Karlyn Kohrs Campbell, *Critiques of Contemporary Rhetoric* (Belmont, California: Wadsworth Publishing Company, Inc., 1972), chapters 2 and 3; and Campbell, "The Nature of Criticism in Rhetorical and Communicative Studies," *The Central States Speech Journal*, 30, 1 (Spring 1979), pp. 4-13.

[2] Kenneth Burke, *A Grammar of Motives* (Berkeley: University of California Press, 1969), p. xv.

[3] For a description of the flexibility of the pentad, see Burke, *A Grammar of Motives*, pp. xv-xxiii.

[4] Burke, *A Grammar of Motives*, p. 3.

[5] Burke, *A Grammar of Motives*, p. 7.

[6] I say "apparently" because the script does not make clear whether Valvert dies or not.

[7] Roger Gross, *Understanding Playscripts: Theory and Method* (Bowling Green, Ohio: Bowling Green University Press, 1974), p. 1.

[8] See "The ATA Wingspread II Conference," edited by Ronald A. Willis, *Theatre News*, XI, 9 (Summer 1979), pp. 13-14.

[9] *Convention '79*, the ATA program for the 1979 convention in New York, p. 39, and *San Diego 1980*, the ATA program for the following year, pp. 25, 35, 38, 39, list panels on performance criticism.

[10] For representative editorial comments, see *Educational Theatre Journal*, 29, 4 (December 1977), p. 466; *Educational Theatre Journal*, 30, 1 (March 1978), p. 4; *Educational Theatre Journal*, 30, 2 (May 1978), p. 150; *The Drama Review*, 21, 4 (December 1977), p. 3.

[11] Roger Gross has raised this question in *theory/crit.*, Spring 1979, an issue of the newsletter of the dramatic theory and criticism interest group of ATA that was devoted largely to performance criticism.

[12] Michael Kirby, "An Introduction," *The Drama Review*, 21 4 (December 1977), p. 3.

[13] Burke, *A Grammar of Motives*, p. 16.

[14] This is an adaptation of an idea of Burke's from *The Rhetoric of Religion: Studies in Logology* (Berkeley: University of California Press, 1970), pp. 16-17.

[15] Again, an adaptation of a passage from Burke, *Language as Symbolic Action*, p. 379.

[16] Here I have used the source cited in note 15, along with p. 378 of the same work.

[17] Burke, "Semantic and Poetic Meaning," in *The Philosophy of Literary Form*, pp. 145-146, also "Terministic Screens" and "What Are the Signs of What?" in *Language as Symbolic Action*, pp. 47, 368-372.

[18] David P. Young, *Something of Great Constancy: The Art of "A Midsummer Night's Dream"* (New Haven: Yale University Press, 1966), p. 89.

[19] M.E. Comtois, "The Hardiness of *A Midsummer Night's Dream*," *Theatre Journal*, 32, 3 (October 1980), p. 306.

[20] Young, pp. 64, 66. The importance of verse forms in the play is also discussed by Ronald Watkins and Jeremy Lemmon, *A Midsummer Night's Dream*, in the *In Shakespeare's Playhouse Series* (Newton Abbot, England: David & Charles, 1974), pp. 27-28, and by P.F. Fisher, "The Argument of *A Midsummer Night's Dream*," *Shakespeare Quarterly*, 8, 3 (Summer 1957), p. 307.

[21] Young, p. 92.

[22] For such a view, see E.K. Chambers, "*A Midsummer Night's Dream*," in *Shakespeare: Modern Essays in Criticism*, edited by Leonard F. Dean (New York: Oxford University Press, 1957), pp. 91-93.

[23] R.W. Dent, "Imagination in *A Midsummer Night's Dream*," *Shakespeare Quarterly*, 15, 2 (Spring 1964), p. 116.

[24] *The Reader's Encyclopedia of Shakespeare*, edited by Oscar James Campbell (New York: Thomas Y. Crowell Company, 1966), pp. 546, 548.

[25] Young, p. 15.

[26] Young, pp. 15-16. Also, Watkins and Lemmon say that the play's "appeal is more to the connoisseur than to the groundlings" (35).

[27] Ronald F. Miller, "*A Midsummer Night's Dream*: The Fairies, Bottom, and the Mystery of Things," *Shakespeare Quarterly*, 26, 3 (Summer 1975), p. 254. The critics mentioned include: C. L. Barber, "May Games and Metamorphoses on a Midsummer Night," in *Shakespeare's Festive Comedy: A Study of Dramatic Form and its Relation to Social Custom* (Princeton: Princeton University Press, 1959), pp. 119-162; Elizabeth Sewell, *The Orphic Voice: Poetry and Natural History* (New Haven: Yale University Press,

1960); Frank Kermode, "The Mature Comedies," in *Early Shakespeare*, Stratford-upon-Avon Studies 3 (New York: St. Martin's, 1961), pp. 214-220; R.W. Dent, cited herein; David P. Young, cited herein; and James Calderwood, "*A Midsummer Night's Dream:* The Illusion of Drama," *Modern Language Quarterly*, 26 (1965), reprinted with alterations as "*A Midsummer Night's Dream:* Art's Illusory Sacrifice," in *Shakespearean Metadrama* (Minneapolis: University of Minnesota Press, 1971), pp. 120-148.

[28] Albert S.G. Canning, *Shakespeare Studied in Eight Plays* (London: T. Fisher Unwin, 1903), pp. 427, 433.

[29] Ernest Schanzer, "The Moon and the Fairies in *A Midsummer Night's Dream*," *University of Toronto Quarterly*, 24, 3 (April 1955), pp. 234, 235, 236.

[30] Dent, p. 116.

[31] Chambers, p. 93.

[32] Young, p. 69. Dent makes the same point, p. 116.

[33] Miller, pp. 258, 264.

[34] Schanzer, p. 241.

[35] Dent, 128.

[36] Chambers, 96.

[37] Dent, p. 126.

[38] Dent, p. 129. See also pp. 124-128.'

[39] For a treatment of the play as actually embodying the structure of a dream, see Comtois' essay.

[40] Miller, 263.

[41] Miller, 263.

[42] Miller, 263.

[43] Miller, 264.

[44] Miller, 264-265.

[45] Miller, 265. If I read Miller correctly, it is ourselves we mourn for here, for just a moment. One recalls Gerard Manley Hopkins' "Spring and Fall," with its extraordinary final line, "It is Margaret you mourn for."

[46] This is the version of the Pauline passage that Dent believes Shakespeare is likely to have been familiar with. See Dent, p. 121.

[47] Miller, p. 267.

[48] Dent, pp. 121-122.

[49] Northrop Frye, from *English Institute Essays*, cited in *The Reader's Encylcopedia of World Drama*, edited by John Gassner and Edward Quinn (New York: Thomas Y. Crowell Company, 1969), p. 1027.

[50] Miller, p. 268.

[51] Miller, p. 268.

[52] This idea is explored at length in *Holy Laughter: Essays on Religion in the Comic Perspective*, edited by M. Conrad Hyers (New York: The Seabury Press, 1969).

[53] The rest of the company: Milo O'Shea as Jamie Cregan, Betty Miller as Deborah, Barry Snider as Mickey Maloy, George Ede as Nicholas Gadsby, Walter Flanagan as Dan Roche, Dermot McNamara as Paddy O'Dowd, and Richard Hamilton as Patch Riley. Setting and Lighting by Ben Edwards. Costumes by Jane Greenwood. Produced by Elliot Martin, by arrangement with the John F. Kennedy Center for the Performing Arts. Production Stage Manager, Mitch Erickson. Casting Consultant, Marjorie Martin.

[54] Walter Kerr, "Vintage O'Neill—But With the Crucial Ambiguity Missing," *The New York Times*, 8 January 1978, Section D, p. 5.

[55] Kerr, p. D5.

[56] Kerr, p. D5.

[57] Kerr, p. D5.

[58] John Simon, "A Touch Is Better Than None," *New York*, January 16, 1978, p. 57.

[59] Simon, p. 57.

[60] Stanley Kauffman, "Arts and Lives," *The New Republic*, January 28, 1978, p. 24.

[61] Kauffman, p. 24.

[62] Kauffman, p. 24.

[63] Kauffman, pp. 24-25.

[64] Kauffman, p. 25.

[65] Frederick I. Carpenter, *Eugene O'Neill*, revised edition (Boston: Twayne Publishers, 1979), p. 146.

[66] John Gassner, *Theatre at the Crossroads: Plays and Playwrights of the Mid-Century American Stage* (New York: Holt, Rinehart and Winston, 1960), p. 239.

[67] Louis Sheaffer, *O'Neill: Son and Artist* (Boston: Little, Brown and Company, 1973), p. 449. This is the second of an impressive two-volume study of O'Neill (the first volume is titled *O'Neill: Son and Playwright*) that provides exhaustive biographical detail about the playwright.

[68] Doris V. Falk, *Eugene O'Neill and the Tragic Tension: An Interpretive Study of the Plays* (New

Brunswick, N.J.: Rutgers University Press, 1958), p. 169.

[69]See, for example, Horst Frenz, *Eugene O'Neill* (New York: Frederick Ungar Publishing Company, 1971), pp. 93-94, and John Henry Raleigh, *The Plays of Eugene O'Neill* (Carbondale: Southern Illinois University Press, 1965), pp. 140, 222-223.

[70]All quotations from the script are from Eugene O'Neill, *A Touch of the Poet* (New Haven: Yale University Press, 1957).

[71]Kerr, p. D5.

[72]Kerr, p. D5.

[73]Frye makes precisely this point regarding several major playwrights. See *Anatomy of Criticism*, pp. 5-6.

[74]Raleigh, pp. 222-223.

[75]Falk, pp. 166-167, 169.

[76]Kerr, p. D5.

[77]Simon, p. 58.

[78]Kauffman, p. 25.

[79]Sheaffer, p. 450.

[80]Falk, p. 169.

[81]Sheaffer, p. 450.

[82]See Raleigh, p. 60.

[83]Sheaffer, p. 450.

[84]Gassner, p. 239.

[85]Robert Brustein, "Theatre Chronicle," *The Hudson Review*, 12, 1 (Spring 1959), p. 97.

[86]*Equus*, written by Peter Schaffer; produced by Kermit Bloomgarden and Doris Cole Abrahams in association with Frank Milton; directed by John Dexter. The play was first performed at the Plymouth Theatre October 24, 1974. The cast included Anthony Hopkins as Martin Dysart, Peter Firth as Alan Strang, Michael Higgins as Frank Strang, Marian Seldes as Hester Salomon, Roberta Maxwell as Jill Mason, Frances Sternhagen as Dora Strang, Walter Mathews as Harry Dalton, Mary Doyle as Nurse, Everett McGill as Horseman/Nugget, and Philip Kraus, John Tyrrell, Gus Kaikkonen, David Ramsey, and Gabriel Oshen as Horses.

[87]Peter Schaffer, *Equus: A Play in Two Acts* (New York: Samuel French, Inc., 1973), pp. 73-74.

[88]I do not wish to claim that performances provide critical standards that are entirely absent from the script, merely that those standards (like the implicit examples on which the text depends) become explicit in the performance, whereas they may be easy to overlook in the playscript.

[89]*A Piece of Monologue*, by Samuel Beckett. Staged by David Warrilow and Michael Kuhling. Cast: Speaker, David Warrilow. Lighting Design, Michael Kuhling. La Mama Etc. 74A East Fourth Street, New York City, December 14-30, 1979. This play may be particularly apt for the performance critic, for it was written specifically for the actor, David Warrilow, and, thus, performance was presumably in the playwright's mind in a very concrete fashion from the inception of the drama.

I chose not to find out whether the actor's voice was recorded or not, although I presume it would have been (perhaps still would be) easy enough to do. The phenomenological reality that the audience faced was that of a mechanical-sounding voice that might well have been recorded, and this effect, this wonder on the part of the audience, was part of the impact of the performance. To discover the facts about the voice would, it seems to me, put the critic in a position no audience member, no matter how sensitive he or she was, could have occupied. The audience had to simply wonder, and it appears to me that the critic must take this wonderment into account.

[91]*Footfalls* and *That Time* can be found in *Ends and Odds: Eight New Dramatic Pieces*, by Samuel Beckett (New York: Grove Press, Inc., 1974). *Play* is part of *Cascando and Other Short Dramatic Pieces*, Samuel Beckett (New York: Grove Press, Inc., 1964). *A Piece of Monologue* is now available in *Rockaby and Other Short Pieces*. New York: Grove Press, Inc., 1981.

[92]For an interesting treatment of this paradox, see Charles R. Lyons, *Samuel Beckett* (London: The Macmillan Press Ltd, 1983), esp. pp. 9-10.

[93]For a very different picture of this production, see Eileen Fischer's review, *Theatre Journal*, 32, 4 (December 1980), p. 534.

[94]Burke, *A Grammar of Motives*, pp. 59-61, 323-401, and especially 323-325.

[95]Burke, *A Grammar of Motives*, p. 326.

[96]It is, I believe, more than coincidental that in the 1960s during the wildest theatrical experimentation, there was really no equivalent of blank art or minimal art in theatre, no equivalent of sculpture in the form of bricks scattered on the floor, no equivalent of music unheard as the pianist sits unmoving before the piano, etc. And it would have been so easy: the so-called theatre piece in which the curtain goes up on a bare stage, the lights very, very slowly come up and then very, very slowly dim out; or

the curtain doesn't rise at all, but the house lights slowly darken and then slowly come up again. It would have been so easy, but these things did not happen in theatre, not because theatre people were conservative or opposed to experimentation, but because theatre *is* theatrical.

Epilogue

In the Prologue and in Chapter I, there was brief mention of talking about the play. Dramatic theory and criticism is just that, the business of talking about performed works: talking about the success or failure of the work or the performance, talking about ways the work might have been performed, and talking about this work and this performance in relation to other performances and other works. Talking to others or to oneself.

There are those who fear that the experience of theatre will be diminished, even destroyed, by such talk. They wish to preserve the excitement and the splendor that can occur when one sees a fine performance. Within certain limits, this attitude should be honored. Frye, for example, talks about the separate processes of experiencing literature and criticism; he says, "The pre-critical experience of literature is wordless,"[1] but criticism, which comes later, is a deliberate and systematic verbal discipline. Hence, one may accept the immediate experience of the work, the theatrical work, as prior to theory and criticism; indeed, Frye says at another point that no one can teach literature, that "the criticism of literature is all that can be directly taught."[2] Frye's statements are as true of theatre as of literature, and they indicate that the danger is not in holding that the experience of the artwork is beyond words; the danger lies in stopping there and refusing to go beyond the wordless experience.

For academicians, the danger is obvious. If we do not talk about theatre, we have nothing to say to our students, and we either go out of business or resort to mute gestures indicating the urgency of this or that sort of unarticulated experience. We must, that is, talk to others.

But I shall not stop there. I want to go beyond Frye and to claim that the experience of theatre is neither pre-critical nor wordless. Instead, one experiences, one perceives the performed work, not in some direct, raw fashion, but via an accumulation of experiences, symbols, beliefs, and convictions about theatre in general, this work in particular, perhaps these actors in other roles, the relations between this work and this performance and similar works and performances. This stance invites ridicule, of course; behind my words looms the spectre of a theatre-goer who quickly catalogues particular line-readings, lighting designs, or what have you and turns them all into a running balance-sheet of a sort; asked what he or she thought of the performance, the only reply would be, "Just a minute, I'll get out my calculator."

The reality is quite different. Viewing, say, *A Midsummer Night's Dream* for the first time, one will screen the performance through a limited number of symbolic structures. But after long experience in the theatre, such issues as the serious dimension of the play, the actors' skill with the verse forms, the deliberate lack of characterization in the four lovers—all these and other items are part of one's experience of the performance. They cannot be set aside, to be donned later on. But it is precisely such acquired symbolic structures that lead one, *not away from the immediate experience, but directly to it.* It is the treasure trove of such past experiences turned into symbolic form that make the great performance so precious to the well-tempered viewer. And it is this process that I believe is properly called critical and that amounts to a form of talking to oneself in critical and theoretical terms; such talk is not a *substitute* for experience or a distortion of experience, but the *enrichment* of experience.

Finally, there are few joys to equal the experience of having known and loved a play, seeing that play in a performance by talented theatre people, seeing the play with someone else who also comes to the performance equipped with a significant past, and then talking about the performance afterwards. It is that sort of talk that is truly heady for dedicated theatre buffs and that, far from leading away from the performance, is likely to drive one back to another performance to see again the richnesses discovered, not during the performance itself, but during the talk afterward. This has ever been the case in my own experience.

Notes

[1]Northrop Frye, *The Critical Path: An Essay on the Social Context of Literary Criticism* (Bloomington: Indiana University Press, 1971), p. 26.

[2]Frye, *Anatomy of Criticism*, p. 11.

Appendix I

Susanne K. Langer's Concept of Form

Susanne Langer's concepts of discursive and presentational form are described in *Philosophy in a New Key* (cited as *PNK* in this appendix), *Problems of Art (PA)*,[1] and *Feeling and Form (FF)*. I want to deal with these concepts here because I do not believe there is any simple, straightforward reading of Langer that does justice to, or even makes complete sense of, these key ideas. That they are key ideas for anyone interested in theatre (or in any of the arts) is, it seems to me, apparent from the fact that the very status of the artwork as a meaningful item, as a symbol, depends on some such ideas; and Langer is the only theorist, to my knowledge, to have worked out a treatment of the artwork as symbol that is both comprehensive (in that it deals with all the arts *and* ties the nature of the art symbol to the fundamental process of symbolization itself) and intensive (in that it deals with each of the arts in considerable detail).

Langer's argument begins with the claim that all items that have meaning or significance or import are *signs*. Signs can be either *signals or symbols*.[2] Signals announce the existence (past, present, or future) of an object or event, and they have a one-to-one relationship with that object or event. Symbols do not refer to the existence of objects or events and bear no one-to-one relationship to them; rather, symbols are "vehicles for the conception of objects" (*PNK*, 60-61). In regard to language, words are occasionally used as signals, but their essential function is symbolic (*PNK*, 57-63).

Signals and symbols have three kinds of meaning: *signification*,[3] in which signals refer to objects or events directly; *symbolization*, which is divided into *denotation* and *connotation: denotation*, a function of symbols in which a subject uses a symbol to stand for a conception, which in turn stands for an object or event; and *connotation*, a second function of symbols in which a subject uses a symbol to stand for a concept not referring to objects or events (*PNK*, 61-64).

All this is part of the logic of terms. By contrast, the logic of connected discourse also includes grammatical structure, which "ties together several symbols, each with at least a fragmentary connotation of its own, to make one complex term whose meaning is a special constellation of all the connotations involved" (*PNK*, 67). That constellation "depends on the syntactical relations within the complex symbol, or proposition" (*PNK*,

68). *"A proposition is a picture of a structure—the structure of a state of affairs"* (*PNK*, 68). These notions of discourse or discursive form and the proposition are vital parts of Langer's argument; she says, "Discursive symbolism, the vehicle of propositional thinking, is essential to any theory of human mentality; for without it there could be no *literal meaning"* (*PNK*, 67).

Langer says the propositions that make up language are meaningful because of a law of projection. That is, language does not simply copy facts; rather, facts are transformed when they are turned into propositions, and they become something like objects which are then named. Thus, "A killed B" simply names three items: A, killing, and B. But via the proper law of projection, such discursive form is understood to mean the action of A killing B (*PNK*, 80).

As in the above example, language (*all* language) has the property of discursiveness or one-after-anotherness. Thus, only that which can be put discursively can be stated verbally (*PNK*, 81). But, writers such as Russell and Carnap to the contrary notwithstanding, this sort of verbal, discursive form is only a tiny part of the symbolic activity in which we all take part (*PNK*, 87-88). There are many things which simply do not fit any grammatical or discursive pattern (*PNK*, 88-89). And that means that a different process, a different symbolic form, must exist and must be used by humans. Evidence that this is so is found in the processes of *formulation* and *abstraction*, via which we organize sensory fields into colors, shapes, sounds, and finally things (*PNK*, 89). And in addition to sounds, shapes, and colors as items we readily turn into symbols, there is the "sense-image," the "more or less stabile form we call a *picture"* (*PNK*, 144), e.g., fire is used as a symbol for passion, a rose as a symbol for beauty (*PNK*, 145). Then there are the sequences of such images (Langer calls them "fantasies" [*PNK*, 146]) we use to record and order subjective experience, e.g., an on-rushing locomotive can be a symbol for danger (*PNK*, 147). That such images and fantasies are, indeed, symbols is indicated by the readiness with which we employ them as metaphors (*PNK*, 145, 147). None of these items is discursive in nature, yet each of them "bears the stamp of mentality" (*PNK*, 90), mentality that exists "whenever the alien world outside impinges on the furthest and smallest receptor" (*PNK*, 90). "The abstractions made by the ear and the eye—the forms of direct perception—are our most primitive instruments of intelligence. They are genuine symbolic materials, media of understanding, by whose office we apprehend a world of *things*, and of events that are the histories of things" (*PNK*, 92).

One may talk of a "language" of colors, shapes, etc., but that term is misleading. First, *"language has a vocabulary and a syntax"* (*PNK*, 94), so that individual elements have at least relatively fixed meanings. Second, in language words are equivalent to certain other words or groups of words, so that single terms can be defined, i.e., we can have dictionaries. Third, in language different words can have the same meaning, and when such samenesses of meaning become systematic, we have different languages and can translate from one to the other (*PNK*, 94). And fourth, in language words have "general reference," i.e., can be used to represent many different objects or events (*PNK*, 96).

But pictures, for example, have no elements with fixed meanings, have no elements that can be defined in terms of other elements, have no elements that can be translated into others, and have no intrinsic generality (they present an individual object or event) *(PNK*, 95-96). Pictures, then, differ in kind from language; they are nondiscursive symbols.

> The meanings given through language are successively understood, and gathered into a whole by the process called discourse; the meanings of all other symbolic elements that compose a larger, articulate symbol are understood only through the meaning of the whole, through their relations within the total structure. Their very functioning as symbols depends on the fact that they are involved in a simultaneous, integral presentation. This kind of semantic may be called "presentational symbolism," to characterize its essential distinction from discursive symbolism, or "language" proper (*PNK*, 97).

It should be noted at this point that Langer intends something rather specific by her terms "language" and "discursive symbolism." It is easy, I think, to misunderstand her to mean that language, sheer verbality, is what is being considered here. The characteristics of fixed meanings, definitions, translations, and general reference all seem to point to language itself as the subject of inquiry. So, too, does the idea of discursiveness regarded as one-after-anotherness, a property common to all language. But there are three terms, and the three ideas they call forth, in the material cited above that make it clear Langer is not applying discursive form to all of language. The terms are syntax, grammar, and proposition. There are many instances of language usage that possess none or only one or two of these characteristics: catalogues, lists, dictionaries; various sorts of poetry which are partly or wholly without syntax; and the great body of fiction which is nonpropositional in nature. Thus, the inference to be drawn at this point is that Langer means by discursive form the standard dictionary meaning, i.e., moving rationally from premises to conclusions. And while her intent may not be entirely clear at this stage, if doubt remains, it is removed quite forcefully later on when she denies that poetry is discursive in nature.

Langer pursues this apparently radical distinction between discursive and presentational form throughout *PNK*, *PA*, and *FF*, working first in the broad areas of language, myth, ritual, and art, and then in each of the major art forms.

All art is made up of presentational forms (*PNK*, 260), and Langer offers a simple definition: "Art is the creation of forms symbolic of human feeling" (*FF*, 40). As I say, this definition seems simple enough, but Langer is quick to point out that those who deal with artistic symbols have always faced paradoxes: form that does not signify, disciplined spontaneity, impersonal feeling, etc. And theorists have often attempted to resolve such paradoxes by using the tactic of combining "opposed ideas by treating them as 'principles' in the classical sense, antithetical characters that may be possessed in varying proportions, opposite poles with a point of perfect balance between them..." (*FF*, 16). But this resort to polarity provides no remedy; feeling and form, for example, are not polar opposites, but "are merely associated, respectively, with each other's negatives" (*FF*, 17). "The conception of polarity, intriguing though it be, is really an unfortunate metaphor whereby a logical muddle is raised to the dignity of a fundamental principle" (*FF*, 17).

Note that this prohibition against the tactic of mixing opposing terms or ideas would appear to prevent any move toward an intermingling of discursive and presentational form, for the two, though radically different, are not in any logical sense polar opposites.

In the symbolic forms called artworks, what is expressed, Langer says, is not actual feeling, but ideas of feeling. In other words, artworks are not emotionally expressive, but logically expressive (*FF*, 67). In expressing these ideas of feeling, the artwork creates a virtual reality, an illusion, a pure semblance; this created reality is not part of the ordinary world, but is given entirely to the senses and/or the mind of the viewer (*FF*, 46ff). And in this process of creating illusions or virtual realities, *materials* (actual items such as paint, canvas, actors' bodies, etc.) are turned into artistic *elements* (virtual items such as a sombre color or a dangerous and menacing figure); it is from the combination or arrangement of these artistic elements that the final illusion is created (*FF*, 84-85).

Once created, "a work of art is a single, indivisible symbol...; it is not, like discourse..., composite, analyzable into more elementary symbols...; a work of art is always a prime symbol" (*FF*, 369).

Note once more the seemingly unbridgable chasm between the presentational form of the artwork and discursive form.

In the poetic arts, literature, film, and drama, the illusion created is that of virtual life or virtual existence, as I indicated in chapter 3. The materials used in these poetic arts include words, but that does not mean at all that the artwork is an instance of discursive form:

Since every poem that is successful enough to merit the name of "poetry"—
regardless of style or category—is a non-discursive symbolic form, it stands to
reason that the laws which govern the making of poetry are not those of
discursive logic. They are "laws of thought" as truly as the principles of
reasoning are; but *they never apply to scientific or pseudo-scientific (practical)
reasoning*. They are, in fact, the laws of imagination. As such they extend over
all the arts, but literature is the field where their differences from discursive
logic become most sharply apparent, because the artist who uses them is using
linguistic forms, and thereby the laws of discourse, at the same time, on another
semantic level (*FF*, 234).

And now, if one has read with close regard to the argument Langer
appears to be building, there is a sharp adjustment to be made. In
literature, *both* the laws of discourse and the laws of imagination are used?
But that would mean that literature involves both discursive and
presentational form, would it not? And if that is the case, what has
happened to the radical difference between the two forms? Some careful
rereading and retracing of one's steps (and Langer's) seems to be in order.

Langer appears to argue that discursive and presentational form differ
in kind, that all art is presentational in nature, and that, therefore, there is
no discursive form in the world of art. But side by side with that argument,
another set of claims is made, and they begin quite early in *PNK*.

Only a chapter after distinguishing between presentational and
discursive form, Langer says that the two general principles underlying the
development of language (which is the major discursive form) are
emendation and *metaphor*. Emendation leads to the fully developed
syntactical structure of language (*PNK*, 138). Metaphor comes into
existence "where a precise word is lacking to designate the novelty which
the speaker would point out, [and] he resorts to the powers of *logical
analogy*, and uses a word denoting something else that is a presentational
symbol for the thing he means" (*PNK*, 139).

Metaphor is our most striking evidence of *abstractive seeing*, of the power
of human minds to use presentational symbols. Every new experience, or new
idea about things, evokes first of all some metaphorical expression. As the idea
becomes familiar, this expression "fades" to a new literal use of the once
metaphorical predicate, a more general use than it had before. It is in this
elementary, presentational mode that our first adventures in conscious
abstraction occur. The spontaneous similes of language are our first record of
similarities perceived.... The use of metaphor can hardly be called a conscious
device. It is the power whereby language, even with a small vocabulary,
manages to embrace a multimillion things; whereby new words are born and
merely analogical meanings become stereotyped into literal definitions....

One might say that, if ritual is the cradle of language, metaphor is the law
of its life. It is the force that makes it essentially *relational*, intellectual, forever
showing up new, abstractable *forms* in reality, forever laying down a deposit of
old, abstracted concepts in an increasing treasure of general words (*PNK*, 141).

I can imagine no reading of this passage (and of others) that does not require one to infer that metaphor is part of language, *all* language. If metaphor is the device whereby we form new meanings, and do so even on the unconscious level, then it can hardly be the case that metaphor is limited to formal or propositional or strictly logical discourse. And metaphor is presentational in form; Langer says so three times, and quite emphatically, in the passages just quoted. At another point, she goes further than that: "A metaphor is not language, it is an idea expressed by language, an idea that in its turn functions as a symbol to express something. It is not discursive and therefore does not really make a statement of the idea it conveys; but it formulates a new conception for our direct imaginative grasp" (*PA*, 23).

The case seems quite clear: language is discursive in nature, but in that it necessarily includes metaphor, it is also presentational in an important sense. Hence the seemingly firm barrier between discursive and presentational form has been breached.

Another breakthrough in the wall dividing the two forms is made shortly. Langer says the difference between discursive and presentational form is not the same as that between literal and artistic meanings. "Many presentational symbols are merely proxy for discourse" (*PNK*, 260), and these include graphs, geometric relations, maps, and diagrams. All these have literal significance and can be translated into discourse.

This breach is not as important as the one created by metaphor. Nevertheless, the combination of metaphor and those symbols that are merely proxy for discourse increases the extent to which presentational and discursive form intermingle.

In regard to specific artforms, the process of interpenetration continues. Langer says, "The material of poetry is discursive, but the product—the artistic phenomenon—is not" (*PNK*, 261). And she adds that, though the poetic form is presentational, it includes literal and propositional sense (*PNK*, 261). One of her strongest statements is the following:

> Language is the material of poetry, but what is done with this material is not what we do with language in actual life; for *poetry is not a kind of discourse at all.*... Its material is language, its motif, or model, usually discursive speech, but what is created is not actual discourse—what is created is a composed and shaped apparition of a new human experience (*PA*, 148).

The poetic use of words is, thus, quite distinct from their communicative function:

> It may be called the *formulative* function of language, which has its own

primitive and advanced, unconscious and conscious levels. It is normally coincident with the communicative functions, but largely independent of them; and while its most spectacular exhibition is in poetry, it is profoundly, though not obviously, operative in our whole language-bound mental life.... The formulative power of words is the source and support of our imagination (*PA*, 148-149).

Poetry is a presentational form that creates its own illusion, but within that form discursive materials are found. And Langer goes beyond the simple mingling of discursive and presentational form when she makes the poetic function of language a part of our mental life; she had earlier described discursive symbolism as "essential to any theory of human mentality." Now presentational symbolism takes its place beside discursive form as indispensable to human intellection.

Langer's argument in the above passages centers on the discursive elements that are part of the presentational form of poetry. But she also reverses matters and describes the presentational elements in discursive form. Non-fiction, she says, is a literary order that includes the essay, philosophy, history, biography, various sorts of reports, and expository writing. "Such writing is in essence not poetry (all poetry is fictive; 'non-fiction' is 'non-poetic'). Yet when it is well done, it meets a standard which is essentially literary, i.e., an artistic standard" (*FF*, 301). Further, "literal, logical thought has a characteristic form, which is known as 'discursive,' because it is the form of discourse. Language is the prime instrument of thought, and the product bears the stamp of the fashioning tool. A writer with literary imagination perceives even this familiar form as a vehicle of feeling" (*FF*, 302).

By this stage, it is apparent that, at least insofar as language is concerned, there is no such thing as pure discursive form. In the presentational forms of the verbal arts, Langer points to the presence of literal sense, of propositional sense; and in the discursive forms of the essay, philosophy, history, etc., she indicates the existence of literary form that meets an artistic standard and is a vehicle of feeling.

Two questions now arise: If discursive and presentational form are not different in kind, as they seemed to be at first, but intermix constantly in language, does Langer provide a conceptual basis on which one can explain this coming together? Or is it simply a matter of juggling things to make sense of the over-all argument? And second, in a mixture of discursive and presentational form, how do individual symbols (be they artworks or single words) *mean*? Do the formulae advanced early in *PNK* still hold?

The answer to the first of these questions is that Langer does, indeed, offer a concept that accounts for the flowing together of the two great symbolic forms. That concept is *assimilation,* a term she uses to explain the ways in which art forms are employed in other art forms, music in theatre, literature in music, etc. Langer holds that every art form assimilates or transforms materials and elements of other arts and uses them for its own purposes. Thus, the words of a song, though they may be poetry in their own right, become musical elements in the song (*FF,* 150). Langer states, "The principle of assimilation holds usually in certain familiar ways. Music ordinarily swallows words and actions creating opera, oratorio, or song; dance commonly assimilates music. But this is not a fast rule. Sometimes a poem may swallow music, or even dance; dramatic poetry quite normally does both" (*PA,* 86). Each art form creates a primary illusion or apparition, and the process of assimilation results in secondary apparitions as well. Virtual space is the primary illusion of the plastic arts and a secondary illusion of music, and time-effects in the plastic arts have the quality of the virtual time of music. "Progressively we find then that the primary apparition of any art may appear as secondary in another, and that in the arts generally all space is plastic space, all time is musical time, all impersonal forces are balletic..., all events poetic" (*PA,* 83-84). And, Langer might have added, all acts dramatic.

Of the theatre in particular, Langer makes this comment in regard to assimilation:

> Drama, on the other hand, swallows all the plastic creations that enter into its theatrical precinct, and their own pictorial, architectural, or sculptural beauties do not add themselves to its own beauty. A great work of sculpture, say the original Venus of Milo that stands in the Louvre, transported to the comic or tragic stage (perhaps in a play about a sculptor) would count only as stage setting, an element in the action, and might not meet this purpose as well as a pasteboard counterfeit of it would do (*PA,* 85).

The concept of assimilation explains the use of one art form by another, but in the process it also explains the use of discursive elements in presentational form. When Langer talks of one art using another, she employs such examples as the words of a song that become poetic elements, and those are discursive materials used in a presentational form. The only difficulty here is that one can easily read Langer to mean that the discursive materials *as such* disappear when assimilated and become artistic elements in the presentational symbol. This, I think, is a misreading, and when Langer says that "poetic reflections...are not essentially trains of logical reasoning, though they may incorporate fragments, at least, of discursive argument" (*FF,* 219), she should be understood to mean that those fragments of argument *exist* and retain their discursive identity, though they take on the functions of artistic elements as well (see also *FF,* 227, 228,

245-246, 256-257). In other words, the materials remain actual, no matter whether they originate in one art form or are borrowed from another.

Finally, there is the question of meaning. In this rather complicated process in which an art form creates its own primary illusion (but may use as a secondary illusion what was primary in a different form) and creates that illusion from its own materials and elements (but may borrow materials and elements from other arts), just how do individual artworks *mean*? Are they in any sense symbols that mean in the way discursive symbols mean? Langer, of course, began by saying that there were three kinds of meaning, signification, denotation, and connotation. But the terms "meaning" and "symbol" undergo changes as Langer's argument proceeds. From the position described above, the position taken early in *PNK*, she moves to the following view at the beginning of *FF:* "A symbol is any device whereby we are enabled to make an abstraction" (*FF*, xi). And from the idea that symbols referred to conceptions of objects or simply to concepts, Langer moves to the position that enables her to make this comment (cited in chapter 3): "The artistic symbol, *qua* artistic, negotiates insight, not reference; it does not rest upon convention, but motivates and dictates conventions" (*FF*, 22).

How did this new state of symbolic affairs come to pass? Because the critical response to *FF* convinced Langer that "the difference between the function of a genuine symbol and a work of art" is great, in fact, "greater than I had realized before" (PA, 126). Langer describes this difference as follows:

> A work of art is an expressive form, and therefore a symbol, but not a symbol which points beyond itself so that one's thought passes on to the concept symbolized. The idea remains bound up in the form that makes it conceivable. That is why I do not call the conveyed, or rather presented, idea the *meaning* of the sensuous form, but use the philosophically less committal word "import" to denote what the sensuous form, the work of art, expresses (*PA*, 67).

The fact that the art symbol does not point beyond itself Langer finds to be of much importance:

> A symbol that cannot be separated from its sense cannot really be said to refer to something outside itself. "Refer" is not the right word for its characteristic function. And when the symbol does not have an accepted reference, the use of it is not properly "communication." Yet its function *is* expression, in the logical, not the biological, sense (*FF*, 380).

With such a statement, Langer recognizes that the very definition of symbol is at issue. She points out that "the great importance of reference and communication by means of symbols has led semanticists to regard these uses as the defining properties of symbols" (*PA*, 132). But Langer's entire argument, from *PNK* on, points away from such a definition:

> That usual definition overlooks the greatest intellectual value and, I think, the prime office of symbols—their power of formulating experience, and presenting it objectively for contemplation, logical intuition, recognition, understanding. That is articulation, or logical expression. And this function every good work of art does perform (*PA*, 132-133).

Hence, "according to the usual definition of 'symbol,' a work of art should not be classed as a symbol at all";[4] yet "the myriad forms of subjectivity, the infinitely complex sense of life, cannot be rendered linguistically, that is, stated," and these forms of subjectivity "are precisely what comes to light in a good work of art" (*PA*, 132, 133).

There is a sense in which this new definition returns to the schemata at the beginning of *PNK*, but not simply to repeat or reinforce what was said there. Langer says the artwork "does not connote a concept or denote its instances" (*PA*, 133), and connotation and denotation were the two kinds of symbolization specified in *PNK*. What the artwork does is something more fundamental: it *formulates* and *abstracts*; it abstracts from experience and it formulates experience so that it can be understood, contemplated, intuited. One might well think that this change in the definition of symbol would require a major reconstruction of the early stages of Langer's argument, but that is not the case. The two terms "formulate" and "abstract" begin to appear early in *PNK*, and to appear in prominent roles. I have already mentioned them in quoted matter, but a few citations (some given previously) will fully reveal their importance:

> "Our merest sense experience is a process of *formulation*" (*PNK*, 89).

> "Our sense-organs make their habitual, unconscious abstractions in the interest of this 'reifying' function that underlies ordinary recognition of objects, knowledge of signals, words, tunes, places, and the possibility of classifying such things in the outer world according to their kind" (*PNK*, 92-93).

> "No symbol is exempt from the office of logical formulation" (*PNK*, 97).

> "The symbolic materials given to our senses...belong to the 'presentational' order. They furnish the elementary abstractions in terms of which ordinary sense-experience is understood" (*PNK*, 98).

> "The formulative power of words is the source and support of our imagination" (*PA*, 149).

"Metaphor is our most striking evidence of *abstractive seeing*, of the power of human minds to use presentational symbols" (*PNK*, 141).

"Images are, therefore, our readiest instruments for abstracting concepts from the tumbling stream of actual impressions" (*PNK*, 145).

Formulation and abstraction have been part of Langer's argument from the beginning. Nevertheless, in changing the meaning of the central term "symbol," Langer adds a new level of meaning to the early part of her argument. She had said that in the logical pattern of signification there were three terms: subject, signal, object. In denotation four terms: subject, symbol, conception, object. And in connotation three terms: subject, symbol, concept. Now one must understand that there are, first of all, two major categories of logical expressiveness: formulation-abstraction and communication. Artistic symbols have the office of formulating and abstracting from experience, and that is all; they do not have separable meaning, and they do not have reference. The communicative function includes three kinds of meaning, but the formulae for those three are somewhat different: signification involves subject, signal, object, and that is unchanged; symbolization is still divided into denotation and connotation, but denotation must now be understood to involve subject, symbol, (formulation-abstraction), conception, object, and connotation now involves subject, symbol, (formulation-abstraction), concept. The addition of the fourth term (or joint term) to the last two formulae does not mean that all symbols are the same as artistic symbols. On the simplest level, artistic symbols are far more complex and highly articulated than are those employed in communication. True, there is a trace of the artistic function that clings to all symbols (and I have used parentheses to indicate that it is but a trace); but there can be no more than a trace, for when communication occurs, the subject attends, not to the symbol, as in the case of art, but to its function. The two great categories of presentational and discursive form remain, of course. They are not precisely equivalent to the functions of formulation-abstraction and communication, though they are nearly so. Presentational symbols fall into the category of formulation-abstraction, except for those that are proxy for discourse; and discursive symbols are communicative in nature, except for the element of literary form, the artistic standard, that even expository writing must meet when it is well done.

Langer has made what might appear to be a radical change in her argument, and the change was made when the argument was well advanced. Ordinarily, one would expect that such a change would entail extensive reworking of early portions of the argument, and there is always the possibility that tampering with an argument as tautly constructed as this one will result in outright chaos. But in this case, one is able to rely on the terms "formulation" and "abstraction" which have been integral parts of Langer's claims from the start. Thus, though a bit of juggling is necessary, the sequence, the line of the argument that Langer has built retains its shapeliness and clarity.

For theatre, Langer's concepts (including the changes I have described) are indispensable. Theatrical works are presentational in form. The many nonverbal and nondiscursive elements of the performed work ensure that, no matter how important the role of language therein, the fundamental form is a presentational one. This is particularly so because the element of language itself always includes a presentational dimension, and may be primarily presentational in nature. Among the artistic elements employed in the theatrical work is discursive form or argument; but this is an element, a dramatic element into which sheerly discursive material has been transformed. Such material retains its identity, but now serves dramatic, i.e., nondiscursive, ends. Hence, when theatre moves too far into the realm of discourse, argument loses its function as a virtual element; it is no longer assimilated into the presentational form, but becomes itself the controlling symbolic form.

In closing, let me simply restate these points: Langer's argument is grounded in the concept of symbolization itself, a grounding that gives her position great logical strength; further, she deals with the major forms of symbolization, language, myth, ritual, and art; and finally, she treats each of the principal art forms in much detail. It would be foolish to say that she has constructed a flawless argument; indeed, some weaknesses are evident. But it is hard to think of a theorist who can rival her in terms of the breadth and depth of the theoretical enterprise undertaken.[5]

Notes

[1]Susanne K. Langer, *Problems of Art: Ten Philosophical Sketches* (New York: Charles Scribner's Sons, 1957).

[2]Langer uses the terms "sign" and "symbol" in *PNK*. But later she changes to "signals" and "symbols," reserving "sign" for the generic term. See *FF*, p. 26, n. 1.

[3]This is the term used in *PNK*, but given the change referred to in the previous note, Langer might prefer "signalization" for this function.

[4]For further comments on the appropriate definition of "symbol," see Susanne K. Langer, *Philosophical Sketches: A Study of the Human Mind in Relation to Feeling, Explored through Art, Language and Symbol* (New York: A Mentor Book, published by arrangement with the Johns Hopkins Press, 1964), pp. 58-61, 80-81.

[5]For negative views of one or more of Langer's key notions, see Ernest Nagel, Review of *Philosophy In A New Key, Journal of Philosophy*, XL (1943), pp. 323-329; Paul Welsh, "Discursive and Presentational Symbols," *Mind*, LXIV (1955), pp. 181-189; Morris Weitz, "Symbolism and Art," *Review of Metaphysics*, VII (1954), pp. 466-481; Kingsley Blake Price, "Is a Work of Art a Symbol?" *The Journal of Philosophy*, L (1953), pp. 485-503.

Appendix II

A PIECE OF MONOLOGUE
Samuel Beckett

Curtain.
Faint diffuse light.
Speaker stands well off centre downstage audience left.
White hair, white nightgown, white socks.
Two metres to his left, same level, same height, standard lamp, skull-sized white globe, faintly lit.
Just visible extreme right, same level, white foot of pallet bed.
Ten seconds before speech begins.
Thirty seconds before end of speech lamplight begins to fail.
Lamp out. Silence. Speaker, globe, foot of pallet, barely visible in diffuse light.
Ten seconds.
Curtain. ·

SPEAKER. Birth was the death of him. Again. Words are few. Dying too. Birth was the death of him. Ghastly grinning ever since. Up at the lid to come. In cradle and crib. At suck first fiasco. With the first totters. From mammy to nanny and back. All the way. Bandied back and forth. So ghastly grinning on. From funeral to funeral. To now. This night. Two and a half billion seconds. Again. Two and a half billion seconds. Hard to believe so few. From funeral to funeral. Funerals of . . . he all but said of loved ones. Thirty thousand nights. Hard to believe so few. Born dead of night. Sun long sunk behind the larches. New needles turning green. In the room dark gaining. Till faint light from standard lamp. Wick turned low. And now. This night. Up at nightfall. Every nightfall. Faint light in room. Whence unknown. None from window. No. Next to none. No such thing as none. Gropes to window and stares out. Stands there staring out. Stock still staring out. Nothing stirring in that black vast. Gropes back in the end to where the lamp is standing. Was standing. When last went out. Loose matches in right-hand pocket. Strikes one on his buttock the way his father taught him. Takes off milkwhite globe and

129

sets it down. Match goes out. Strikes a second as before. Takes off chimney. Smoke-clouded. Holds it in left hand. Match goes out. Strikes a third as before and sets it to wick. Puts back chimney. Match goes out. Puts back globe. Turns wick low. Backs away to edge of light and turns to face east. Blank wall. So nightly. Up. Socks. Nightgown. Window. Lamp. Backs away to edge of light and stands facing blank wall. Covered with pictures once. Pictures of . . . he all but said of loved ones. Unframed. Unglazed. Pinned to wall with drawing-pins. All shapes and sizes. Down one after another. Gone. Torn to shreds and scattered. Strewn all over the floor. Not at one sweep. No sudden fit of . . . no word. Ripped from the wall and torn to shreds one by one. Over the years. Years of night. Nothing on the wall now but the pins. Not all. Some out with the wrench. Some still pinning a shred. So stands there facing blank wall. Dying on. No more no less. No. Less. Less to die. Ever less. Like light at nightfall. Stands there facing east. Blank pinpocked surface once white in shadow. Could once name them all. There was father. That grey void. There mother. That other. There together. Smiling. Wedding day. There all three. That grey blot. There alone. He alone. Not now. Forgotten. All gone so long. Gone. Ripped off and torn to shreds. Scattered all over the floor. Swept out of the way under the bed and left. Thousand shreds under the bed with the dust and spiders. All the . . . he all but said the loved ones. Stands there facing the wall staring beyond. Nothing there either. Nothing stirring there either. Nothing stirring anywhere. Nothing to be seen anywhere. Nothing to be heard anywhere. Room once full of sounds. Faint sounds. Whence unknown. Fewer and fainter as time wore on. Nights wore on. None now. No. No such thing as none. Rain some nights still slant against the panes. Or dropping gentle on the place beneath. Even now. Lamp smoking though wick turned low. Strange. Faint smoke issuing through vent in globe. Low ceiling stained by night after night of this. Dark shapeless blot on surface elsewhere white. Once white. Stands facing wall after the various motions described. That is up at nightfall and into gown and socks. No. In them already. In them all night. All day. All day and night. Up at nightfall in gown and socks and after a moment to get his bearings gropes to window. Faint light in room. Unutterably faint. Whence unknown. Stands stock still staring out. Into black vast. Nothing there. Nothing stirring. That he can see. Hear. Dwells thus as if unable to move again. Or no will left to move again. Not enough will left to move again. Turns in the end and gropes to where he knows the lamp is standing. Thinks he knows. Was last standing. When last went out. Match one as described for

globe. Two for chimney. Three for wick. Chimney and globe back on.
Turns wick low. Backs away to edge of light and turns to face wall.
East. Still as the lamp by his side. Gown and socks white to take faint
light. Once white. Hair white to take faint light. Foot of pallet just
visible edge of frame. Once white to take faint light. Stands there
staring beyond. Nothing. Empty dark. Till first word always the
same. Night after night the same. Birth. Then slow fade up of a faint
form. Out of the dark. A window. Looking west. Sun long sunk
behind the larches. Light dying. Soon none left to die. No. No such
thing as no light. Starless moonless heaven. Dies on to dawn and
never dies. There in the dark that window. Night slowly falling. Eyes
to the small pane gaze at that first night. Turn from it in the end to
face the darkened room. There in the end slowly a faint hand.
Holding aloft a lighted spill. In light of spill faintly the hand and
milkwhite globe. Then second hand. In light of spill. Takes off globe
and disappears. Reappears empty. Takes off chimney. Two hands
and chimney in light of spill. Spill to wick. Chimney back on. Hand
with spill disappears. Second hand disappears. Chimney alone in
gloom. Hand reappears with globe. Globe back on. Turns wick low.
Pale globe alone in gloom. Glimmer of brass bedrail. Fade. Birth the
death of him. That nevoid smile. Thirty thousand nights. Stands at
edge of lamplight staring beyond. Into dark whole again. Window
gone. Hands gone. Light gone. Gone. Again and again. Again and
again gone. Till dark slowly parts again. Grey light. Rain pelting.
Umbrellas round a grave. Seen from above. Streaming black
canopies. Black ditch beneath. Rain bubbling in the black mud.
Empty for the moment. That place beneath. Which . . . he all but
said which loved one? Thirty seconds. To add to the two and a half
billion odd. Then fade. Dark whole again. Blest dark. No. No such
thing as whole. Stands staring beyond half hearing what he's saying.
He? The words falling from his mouth. Making do with his mouth.
Lights lamp as described. Backs away to edge of light and turns to
face wall. Stares beyond into dark. Waits for first word always the
same. It gathers in his mouth. Parts lips and thrusts tongue forward.
Birth. Parts the dark. Slowly the window. That first night. The room.
The spill. The hands. The lamp. The gleam of brass. Fade. Gone.
Again and again gone. Mouth agape. A cry. Stifled by nasal. Dark
parts. Grey light. Rain pelting. Streaming umbrellas. Ditch. Bubbling
black mud. Coffin out of frame. Whose? Fade. Gone. Move on to
other matters. Try to move on. To other matters. How far from wall?
Head almost touching. As at window. Eyes glued to pane staring out.
Nothing stirring. Black vast. Stands there stock still staring out as if

unable to move again. Or gone the will to move again. Gone. Faint cry in his ear. Mouth agape. Closed with hiss of breath. Lips joined. Feel soft touch of lip on lip. Lip lipping lip. Then parted by cry as before. Where is he now? Back at window staring out. Eyes glued to pane. As if looking his last. Turns away at last and gropes through faint unaccountable light to unseen lamp. White gown moving through that gloom. Once white. Lights and moves to face wall as described. Head almost touching. Stands there staring beyond waiting for first word. It gathers in his mouth. Parts lips and thrusts tongue between them. Tip of tongue. Feel soft touch of tongue on lips. Of lips on tongue. Stare beyond through rift in dark to other dark. Further dark. Sun long sunk behind the larches. Nothing stirring. Nothing faintly stirring. Stock still eyes glued to pane. As if looking his last. At that first night. Of thirty thousand odd. Where soon to be. This night to be. Spill. Hands. Lamp. Gleam of brass. Pale globe alone in gloom. Brass bedrail catching light. Thirty seconds. To swell the two and a half billion odd. Fade. Gone. Cry. Snuffed with breath of nostrils. Again and again. Again and again gone. Till whose grave? Which . . . he all but said which loved one's? He? Black ditch in pelting rain. Way out through the grey rift in dark. Seen from on high. Streaming canopies. Bubbling black mud. Coffin on its way. Loved one . . . he all but said loved one on his way. Her way. Thirty seconds. Fade. Gone. Stands there staring beyond. Into dark whole again. No. No such thing as whole. Head almost touching wall. White hair catching light. White gown. White socks. White foot of pallet edge of frame stage left. Once white. Least . . . give and head rests on wall. But no. Stock still head haught staring beyond. Nothing stirring. Faintly stirring. Thirty thousand nights of ghosts beyond. Beyond that black beyond. Ghost light. Ghost nights. Ghost rooms. Ghost graves. Ghost . . . he all but said ghost loved ones. Waiting on the rip word. Stands there staring beyond at that black veil lips quivering to half-heard words. Treating of other matters. Trying to treat of other matters. Till half hears there are no other matters. Never were other matters. Never two matters. Never but the one matter. The dead and gone. The dying and the going. From the word go. The word begone. Such as the light going now. Beginning to go. In the room. Where else? Unnoticed by him staring beyond. The globe alone. Not the other. The unaccountable. From nowhere. On all sides nowhere. The globe alone. Alone gone.

Index

Index